HAVE A G.R.E.A.T. DAY

HAVE A G.R.E.A.T. DAY

Living Our Lives One Blessed Day at a Time

With Additional Study Helps

Dr. James M. Cecy

JARON Ministries International, Inc.

Jesus' Ambassadors Reaching Out to Nations

Equipping Leaders for Effective Service

Copyright 2020 by Dr. James M. Cecy. All rights reserved.

No part of this publication may be reproduced, stored in a retrieval system, or transmitted, in any form or by any means, electronic, mechanical, photocopying or otherwise, without prior written permission from JARON Ministries International, Inc.

To order this book, visit www.jaron.org or www.puritywar.com or www.amazon.com.

ISBN 978-1-7357365-0-1 PAPERBACK
ISBN 978-1-7357365-1-8 eBOOK
Library of Congress Control Number: 2020923034

Unless otherwise noted, Scriptures are taken from the NEW AMERICAN STANDARD BIBLE (NASB), Copyright © 1960, 1962, 1963, 1968, 1971, 1972, 1973, 1975, 1977, 1995 by THE LOCKMAN FOUNDATION. A Corporation Not for Profit, LA HABRA, CA. All Rights Reserved. Used by permission. http://www.lockman.org.

Some passages are taken from The New International (NIV) Version ® Copyright THE HOLY BIBLE, NEW INTERNATIONAL VERSION® NIV ® Copyright © 1973, 1978, 1984 by International Bible Society® Used by permission. All rights reserved worldwide.

Transliterations and definitions of all Greek and Hebrew words were taken from a variety of sources such as *The Exhaustive Concordance of the Bible* by James Strong, *An Expository Dictionary of New Testament Words* by W.E. Vine, *An Expository Dictionary of Old Testament Words* by F.F. Bruce, Concordance – International Standard Bible Encyclopaedia" Blue Letter Bible. https||www.blueletterbible.org|search|dictionary|ViewTopic.cfm, as well as the author's preferred transliterations to allow for ease of pronunciation.

The author has taken the liberty to capitalize, italicize or underline some portions of Scriptures for emphasis. He has also added in brackets or parentheses some clarifying notes. It is to be understood these, unless otherwise noted, were not in the original translations.

Portions of this book, especially in the appendices, are adapted from a variety of Dr. Cecy's audio, video and written publications. For further information about media and seminars, contact:

>JARON Ministries International, Inc.,
>4710 N Maple Ave, Fresno, CA. 93726
>(559) 227-7997

JARON Ministries International, Inc. is a registered non-profit organization (501c3) in the State of California.

JARON Ministries website: www.jaron.org.

Dr. Cecy's website: www.puritywar.com.

Campus Bible Church website: www.campusbiblechurch.com.

Published by JARON Ministries International, Inc.

Printed in the United States of America.

Cover photo credit: Tini Nguyen

DEDICATION

Unum Diem ad Tempus (One Day at a Time)

To My Precious Lord Jesus Christ

One day at a time, since 1971, You have taught me that You are "the same, yesterday and today and forever" (Hebrews 13:8). I dedicate the remaining days of my life to You, Lord Jesus. Do with them what You will.

To My Precious Wife, Karon Marie

One day at a time, since 1973, you have been by my side as an intimate friend and Christ-centered partner in this amazing journey. May God give us many more years to serve Him together.

To My Precious Children and Grandchildren

One day at a time, since 1978, when our first child arrived, we have joyfully watched our "unexpected" generations unfold. May you all be devoted Christ-followers and world-changers.

To My Precious Team at JARON Ministries International

One day at a time, since 1990, you have taught me what a heart for the world looks like. I am honored to serve with you in these challenging days of global ministry.

To My Precious People at Campus Bible Church

One day at a time, since 1995, you have patiently and lovingly allowed me to grow as a Shepherd and Pastor-Teacher. I am excited about the future as people from all walks of life "Come…Grow…and Go!"

CONTENTS

DEDICATION   7

PREFACE   11

INTRODUCTION: 15
    I Want to "Today" Well

CHAPTER ONE: 25
    G = GREET the day with PRAISE

CHAPTER TWO: 43
    R = REPORT to the day with PURPOSE

CHAPTER THREE: 59
    E = ENGAGE the day with a PLAN

CHAPTER FOUR: 69
    A = ANALYZE the day with PERSPECTIVE

CHAPTER FIVE: 77
    T = TERMINATE the day with PRAYER

CONCLUSION: The Beginning of the Journey   83
    "Carpe Diem: Seize the Day"

APPENDICES

APPENDIX ONE: Personal and Group Study Guide   91

APPENDIX TWO: Preparing My Heart to Worship Daily (An Overview of Psalm 95)   93

APPENDIX THREE: Developing a Heart for Morning Devotion (An Overview of Psalm 5:1-3)   99

APPENDIX FOUR: Alphabetical Worship Worksheet   103

APPENDIX FIVE: Worksheet for Resolving a Conflict 105

APPENDIX SIX: God Has Spoken in His Marvelous Word (An Overview of Psalm 19:7-14) 109

APPENDIX SEVEN: Principles for Effective P.R.A.Y.E.R. 115

APPENDIX EIGHT: Roadblocks to an Effective Prayer-Life 117

APPENDIX NINE: Daily Bible Reading Ideas 127

APPENDIX TEN: A Pocket Guide to Effective Bible Study 129

APPENDIX ELEVEN: My Daily Prayer Journal 131

APPENDIX TWELVE: My Daily Priority List 133

APPENDIX THIRTEEN: How Do I Make Biblical Decisions Every Day? 135

APPENDIX FOURTEEN: Developing My Life Focus 139

APPENDIX FIFTEEN: My Daily Accountability Worksheet 145

APPENDIX SIXTEEN: The A.C.T.S. of Repentance 147

ABOUT THE AUTHOR 149

ABOUT JARON MINISTRIES INTERNATIONAL 151

SCRIPTURE INDEX 153
  • Foreign Language Index

OTHER BOOKS BY DR. JIM CECY 161

PREFACE

The purpose of a preface is to share the author's intention for writing, especially when it comes to things that are unusual or unique. I have chosen to do this in the form of answers to questions you might ask:

Why did you write this book?

My philosophy has been to write books containing precepts and principles that have a proven track record. They are not merely theoretical or theological. I am pleased to share these practical guidelines that have changed my life over the decades. It is my fervent prayer they will also help bring order to your daily life.

Why did you use acrostics and acronyms?
(e.g. G.R.E.A.T., P.R.A.Y.E.R., etc.)

Acrostics and acronyms are familiar and useful memory devices, even used in Old Testament literature. For example, Psalm 119 is a lengthy acrostic using one of the twenty-two letters of the Hebrew alphabet to begin each section. This was most likely done to assist in remembering this psalm, the longest chapter in the Bible. This is also the form used in the entire Book of Lamentations.

Today, we find acrostics and acronyms equally helpful. Many have used the pneumonic device for remembering key aspects of daily prayer (A.C.T.S = Adoration. Confession. Thanksgiving. Supplication.)

Arguably, acrostics and acronyms only work in the original language of the author. I am grateful English has become the international language, spoken by many as a second language. As they have always done with foreign translations of my books and materials, I expect my non-English-speaking brothers and sisters will come up with their own wonderful adaptations.

Why are there so many Scriptures in this little book?

I have chosen to use a large number of Scriptures, many more than normal for a book this size. My intentions are to drive us back to the Bible, the only perfectly reliable source of faith and practice (cf. 2 Timothy 3:16). Certainly, I hope my explanations, principles, anecdotes and stories are helpful, but only the Word of God has the life-changing power to change our lives—from the inside out and far beyond my reach:

> For the word of God is living and active and sharper than any two-edged sword, and piercing as far as the division of soul and spirit, of both joints and marrow, and able to judge the thoughts and intentions of the heart (Hebrews 4:12).

> The words of wise men are like goads, and masters of these collections (i.e. the Word of God) are like well-driven nails; they are given by one Shepherd (Ecclesiastes 4:11).

Why are most of the Scriptures written out rather than just referenced?

Most of us, when reading books other than the Word of God, rarely take the time to look up the Bible references mentioned by the authors. We make assumptions the verses are accurately interpreted and applied. However, that may or may not be true.

PREFACE

My heart is to have each of us approach this book in the spirit of the noble-minded Bereans, who eagerly received the word from the great apostle Paul, but nonetheless examined the Scriptures to see whether what he said was true to the Word of God (cf. Acts 17:11). I expect no less from my astute readers.

Why did you primarily use the New American Standard Bible?

After fifty years of ministry, this is the English translation with which I am most familiar. I have also found this version to be greatly appreciated by scholars for its accuracy of translation from the Hebrew, Aramaic and Greek texts. This is not to say I believe it is the easiest to read. I encourage you to use other fine translations to help bring clarification to the texts, especially if English is your second language.

Why is almost half the book study questions, worksheets and other studies?

I realize this is highly unusual, as well. It is my desire to provide a number of tools that will enhance the precepts and principles laid out in this book. Like any tool chest, they are there if you need them now or in the future.

Finally, in the writing of this book, I have taken to heart the words of King Solomon: "The Preacher sought to find delightful words and to write words of truth correctly" (Ecclesiastes 12:10). May it be so.

Soli Deo Gloria (Glory to God alone)

Dr. Jim Cecy
Fresno, California

INTRODUCTION

I WANT TO "TODAY" WELL

I recall the delightful story of two psychologists who passed each other walking down the street. *"Good morning,"* said the first, to which the second mumbled under his breath, *"I wonder what he meant by that?"*

What does it really mean to wish someone a *"Good morning"* and encourage them to *"Have a great day"*? I remember the scene from an old movie, where the leading man said to the leading lady, *"Have a great life."* What exactly is a great life? I suppose one could say a great life is one that is filled with great days.

The Bible speaks of King David's life as "full of days" (1 Chronicles 29:28). That was also true of Abraham (Genesis 25:8), Isaac (Genesis 35:29) and Job (Job 42:17). The word translated "full" is the Hebrew word *sabea'* which speaks of days that are "abounding with satisfaction." Isn't that a wonderful way to describe a life well-lived? Yet, a life that is "full of days" is really the sum total of a whole bunch of days lived out *unum diem ad tempus*—one day at a time. For me, the total of my days here on Earth is well over 25,000! If I lived in the 18th century I would be boasting to the younger generation, "Many moons have passed."

Given my family history of early deaths, this is quite remarkable. Remembering some of the risky things I did in my young and foolish years, it really is a miracle. I suspect I wore out a few guardian angels. Reading the life of King David, I cannot even imagine how many of the heavenly host applied for early retirement!

"TEMPUS FUGIT: TIME FLIES"

Psalm 90 was written by Moses, the man of God, when he was about eighty years old. It could well be titled, "The Old Man's Psalm." Let's consider a few verses written by a man who knew his days were numbered:

> ... from everlasting to everlasting, You are God (Psalm 90:2).
>
> For a thousand years in Your sight are like yesterday when it passes by, or as a watch in the night (Psalm 90:4).
>
> As for the days of our life, they contain seventy years, or if due to strength, eighty years ... (Psalm 90:10).
>
> So teach us to number our days, that we may present to You a heart of wisdom (Psalm 90:12).
>
> O satisfy us in the morning with Your lovingkindness, that we may sing for joy and be glad all our days (Psalm 90:14).

Moses reminds us that whereas our eternal God is not bound by time and space, our lives on earth are. He observes that a typical man's life is seventy years, maybe eighty, if we are strong. Perhaps we will live to ninety or over a hundred, if we are even healthier. Now that I am seventy years old, it makes me ponder more and more the passages related to my mortality and yours:

INTRODUCTION

... for we were born only yesterday and know nothing and our days on earth are but a shadow (Job 8:9, New International Version).

Man ... is short-lived .... his days are determined. The number of his months is with You .... (Job 14:1, 5).

My times are in Your hands (Psalm 31:15).

Show me, LORD, my life's end and the number of my days. Let me know how fleeting my life is (Psalm 39:4, New International Version).

Do not cast me off in the time of old age; do not forsake me when my strength fails (Psalm 71:9).

... childhood and the prime of life are fleeting (Ecclesiastes 11:10).

Yet you do not know what your life will be like tomorrow. You are just a vapor that appears for a little while and then vanishes away (James 4:14).

Consider elderly Moses' exhortation in Psalm 90 again: "So teach us to *number our days*, that we may present to You a heart of wisdom" (Psalm 90:12). Is he saying that life is just a matter of numbering the days we have lived and those we hope we might have left? Or is he saying to make the most of the days we have on this earth? I think you would agree with the latter. In the New Testament the apostle Paul spoke of making the most of each day's opportunities and redeeming the precious time we have left (cf. Colossians 4:5; Ephesians 5:16).

I once read the average person who lives to seventy years of age spends over twenty years sleeping, twenty years working, and six years eating. I can't imagine how many years are spent trying to find that ubiquitous but elusive mobile phone. *Tempus fugit*: Time flies. Apparently, so do my car keys!

I want us to think about this expression: *"Have a great day!"* I have attempted to examine many of the Bible references dealing with living life one day at a time, as well as living those numbered days well enough to enjoy a full life that is "abounding in satisfaction." I am motivated by the profound words God spoke to His people as they were preparing to take their first steps into the Promised Land:

> See, I have set before you *today* life and prosperity, and death and adversity (Deuteronomy 30:15).

We can have good days, filled with life and prosperity and bad days, filled with death and adversity. We can also have days that can seem like we moved three steps forward, one step sideways and one step backwards. Do the math. At least we are progressing. Even the smallest steps in the right direction can turn out to be some of the biggest steps of our lives.

Throughout the Bible we find the challenge to choose wisely how we will spend each day:

> . . . choose for yourselves *today* whom you will serve . . . . but as for me and my house, we will serve the LORD (Joshua 24:15).

INTRODUCTION

YESTERDAY AND TOMORROW

In the 1960s, Paul McCartney, member of the Beatles rock band, wrote a song entitled, "*Yesterday.*" Perhaps you recall a few of the opening lines:

> *Yesterday, all my troubles seemed so far away.*
> *Now it looks as though they're here to stay.*
> *Oh, I believe in yesterday.*
> *Suddenly, I'm not half the man I used to be.*
> *There's a shadow hangin' over me.*
> *Oh, yesterday came suddenly.*

The words imply that the yesterday that came and went so suddenly left behind many unresolved troubles that are still overshadowing us today, so much so, we wish today was yesterday. This reminds me of what Jesus preached in His Sermon on the Mount, when He warned the crowds:

> . . . do not worry about tomorrow; for tomorrow will care for itself. Each day has enough trouble of its own (Matthew 6:34).

I once read: "Yesterday is a canceled check. Tomorrow is a promissory note. Today is the only cash we have. Spend it wisely." Sound advice!

It brings to mind the century-old words from a poem written by the renowned British missionary, C.T. Studd: "Only one life, 'twill soon be past. Only what's done for Christ will last."

It also makes me want to sing a familiar old song, co-written by Marijohn Wilkin and Kris Kristofferson around the time I began to follow Christ:

> *One day at a time, sweet Jesus.*
> *That's all I'm asking from You.*
> *Just give me the strength,*
> *To do every day what I have to do.*
> *Yesterday's gone, sweet Jesus,*
> *And tomorrow may never be mine.*
> *Lord, help me today. Show me the way,*
> *One day at a time.*

I am just as motivated by the beginning lyrics of a more recent chorus, sung by Jeremy Camp:

> *. . . oh Lord, keep me in the moment,*
> *Help me live with my eyes wide open,*
> *'Cause I don't wanna miss what You*
> *have for me.*

"TODAY" IS AN ACTION VERB

Today really is the first day of the rest of our lives—a day when we can choose the road to life and prosperity or the road to death and adversity. In other words, life is the sum total of the choices we make each day. It is almost as if, biblically-speaking, today is an action verb calling us to declare:

> "Lord, I may not have YESTERDAY-ED well. I may not TOMORROW well. But I choose to TODAY well."

How does one spend today wisely? How does one go about having a great day that makes for a great life, no matter what happens? I want to present to you some daily guidelines I designed for myself many years ago.

INTRODUCTION

PRINCIPLES FOR HAVING A G.R.E.A.T. DAY

One of my earliest recollections of attending church is snuggling up to my mother's fox stole (I still remember those freaky glass eyes!). My mind is often flooded with the memory of her sweet voice singing, *"Holy, holy, holy. Lord, God Almighty. Early in the morning, our song shall rise to Thee."*
    It has been well said that worship is the adoring response of the creature (us) to the infinite majesty of the Creator (God). I believe we could spend a lifetime meditating on His greatness expressed in so many ways. I am struck by the following verses:

> The LORD's lovingkindnesses ("steadfastness, love and loyalty," Hebrew: *hesed*) indeed never cease, for His compassions never fail. They are new ("fresh," Hebrew: *khadash*) every morning. GREAT is Your faithfulness (Lamentations 3:22-23).

> For the LORD is a GREAT God and a GREAT king above all gods (Psalm 95:13).

> GREAT is the LORD and GREATLY to be praised (Psalm 96:4).

    One morning, while reflecting on this wonderful theme, I put together an acrostic to remind myself of how to order each of my days in a way that would be pleasing to the Great One who is holy, holy, holy! It has been a simple and effective tool I have used for decades. I pray it will be a help for many of your todays, as well:

G = GREET the day with PRAISE.
R = REPORT to the day with PURPOSE.
E = ENGAGE the day with a PLAN.
A = ANALYZE the day with PERSPECTIVE.
T = TERMINATE the day with PRAYER.

In the following chapters, we will take a closer and more personal look at each of these. I also encourage you to carefully read Appendix Two: "Preparing My Heart to Worship Daily (An Overview of Psalm 95)."

Welcome to the joy of living our lives one blessed day at a time. I love the words taken from the diary of Jim Elliot, who was martyred for his faith in Christ:

> *"God, I pray Thee, light these idle sticks of my life, that I may burn for Thee. Consume my life, my God, for it is Thine. I seek not a long life, but a full one, like You, Lord Jesus."*

INTRODUCTION

TODAY'S ASSIGNMENTS

1. Who do you know that has lived a life "full of days?" What qualities are most intriguing to you?

2. Calculate how many days you have lived and how many days you have left if you live to one hundred years old?

• I have lived approximately _____ days.

• If I live to a hundred, I have approximately _____ days left.

3. Reflect on Lamentations 3:22-23 "The LORD's lovingkindnesses indeed never cease, for His compassions never fail. They are new every morning. Great is Your faithfulness."

What expressions of God's steadfast love and loyalty (i.e. His lovingkindnesses) are new and fresh for you <u>today</u>?

4. Memorize the Principles for Having a G.R.E.A.T. Day:

       G = GREET the day with PRAISE.
       R = REPORT to the day with PURPOSE.
       E = ENGAGE the day with a PLAN.
       A = ANALYZE the day with PERSPECTIVE.
       T = TERMINATE the day with PRAYER.

TOMORROW'S OPPORTUNITIES

1. Read Appendix Two: "Preparing My Heart to Worship Daily (An Overview of Psalm 95)."

2. Read Hebrews, Chapters 3 and 4 regarding what it means to "enter His rest." Describe how that applies to your daily activities:

CHAPTER ONE

G = GREET the day with PRAISE

"An hour in the morning is worth two in the evening. While the dew is on the grass, let grace drop upon the soul. Let us give to God the mornings of our days and the mornings of our lives" (Charles Haddon Spurgeon).

I will awaken the dawn (Psalm 108:2).

It is good to give thanks to the LORD and to sing praises to Your name, O Most High; to declare Your lovingkindness in the morning . . . (Psalm 92:1-2).

. . . I will be satisfied with Your likeness ("form, attributes," Hebrew: *temunah*) when I awake (Psalm 17:15).

I rise before dawn and cry for help; I wait for Your words (Psalm 119:147).

Let the morning bring me word of your unfailing love, for I have put my trust in you. Show me the way I should go, for to you I entrust my life (Psalm 143:8, New International Version).

In the early morning, while it was still dark, Jesus got up, left the house, and went away to a secluded place, and was praying there (Mark 1:35).

Next to my chair where I pray and read my Bible, I framed the words of Jesus to His weary disciples in the Garden of Gethsemane on the night He was arrested:

> Why are you sleeping? Get up and pray . . . (Luke 22:46).

Some of us are just not morning people. Instead of "Good morning, Lord!" it's "Good Lord, it's morning!" We are rather like Eeyore, the moody donkey in the Winnie the Pooh series, often crying out in a deep-throated whine, "Oh, no, it's another day." Others of us are like Tigger, the hyper-active tiger. At daybreak, we are ready to pounce on the day. Bouncy. Bouncy.

I'm a Tigger and it drives my wife crazy. I often wake up with a cheerful, "Hi honey. What's the plan today!" Her response is usually, "The plan is to let me sleep—at least until the sun comes up!" (I am not suggesting she's an Eeyore. Then again, most people are at 5 a.m.). I suspect one of her favorite proverbs is:

> He who blesses his friend (e.g. his wife) with a loud voice early in the morning, it will be reckoned a curse to him (Well, certainly not a blessing) (Proverbs 27:14, my additions).

Even if we are morning people, it is so easy to wake up and begin the day consumed with the anxieties related to the activities of the day ahead of us. It can immobilize us, even before the day begins.

Comedian Jim Gaffigan rightly observed what is a familiar morning practice: "Nothing like starting the day with a little procrastination." That's not beginning our day with a heavenly perspective.

G = GREET the day with PRAISE

The Psalmist, quite possibly Moses during the difficult days of the Exodus, reminds us:

> This is the day the LORD has made; let us rejoice and be glad in it (Psalm 118:24).

He is saying we are to rejoice in every new day, praising God for the exciting opportunities, even in old and troublesome circumstances. In our wilderness journeys, we are *to rejoice and be glad.*

That's quite a challenge, especially when we understand what these words mean. The word translated *rejoice* is the Hebrew word *gil* and it speaks of shouting out with joy. The expression *be glad* comes from the Hebrew word *samach* which, quite literally, means to cheer. Both words put together give the idea of shouting out (not at the kids or the pets) and cheering the day. I recently read: "Jumping for joy is good exercise."

Okay, maybe cheering and shouting is not our thing in the morning. At least entertain another option from the Psalms: The Songbook of the People of God:

> Awake my glory! Awake, harp and lyre (i.e. musical instruments)! I will awaken the dawn. I will give thanks to You, O LORD . . .
> (Psalm 57:8-9).

Yes, I shall *joyfully sing* Your lovingkindness in the morning (Psalm 59:16).

As believers who have a great and powerful God in charge of our lives, we can celebrate and cheer the new day, using the instrument of our voices to sing our praises even before the day starts. I am not suggesting we stand outside and serenade our neighbors, but I think we get the idea. We are to begin the day with the understanding that our Heavenly Father is the Sovereign Lord, the Creator and the One in charge of the details of our lives. Therefore, He can handle today for us. For this we praise Him, no matter what we are about to encounter. We can cry out daily, "Lord, God Almighty, this is going to be a great day because You made this day for me." Admittedly, for some of us "control-freaks" that may require resigning as General Manager of the Universe!

> "Lord, I choose to stand and cheer the day. You are on Your throne. Take charge of my life today!"

LOVE HIM IN THE MORNING

I love King David's morning prayer in Psalm 139. After elaborating on the wonder of God's presence <u>with him</u>, David ends with a declaration of his presence <u>with God</u>:

> When I awake I am still <u>with You</u>
> (Psalm 139:18).

It reminds me of the many wonderful passages in the Bible showing how accessible our great God is:

> God is our refuge and strength, a very present help in trouble (Psalm 46:1).

> . . . the nearness of God is my good . . .
> (Psalm 73:28).

> Draw near to God and He will draw near to you . . . (James 4:8).

G = GREET the day with PRAISE

. . . let us draw near with confidence to the throne of grace, so that we may receive mercy and find grace to help in time of need (Hebrews 4:16).

. . . let us draw near with a sincere heart in full assurance (Hebrews 10:22).

I am blessed by the words of the second stanza of the old hymn, *Day by Day*, written in 1865 by Lina Sandell, several years after she witnessed the tragic drowning of her father. The song begins:

Day by day and with each passing moment,
Strength I find to meet my trials here.

I am especially prompted in my daily activities to consider the words from the second stanza:

Every day the Lord Himself is near me,
With a special mercy for each hour.
All my cares He fain would bear and cheer me,
He whose name is Counselor and Power.

In Appendix Three I have laid out an overview of Psalm 5:1-3 entitled, "Developing a Heart for Morning Devotions." It presents seven principles I encourage you to mull over in more detail later. Let me just highlight them now:

- **Morning Devotion Principle #1. Wake up aware that God wants to hear from you.**

    Give ear to my words, O LORD . . .
    (Psalm 5:1a).

- **Morning Devotion Principle #2. Share with God your deepest feelings every morning.**

    Consider my groaning (Psalm 5:1b).

- **Morning Devotion Principle #3. Be honest about what you really need.**

    Heed the sound of my cry for help, my King and my God . . . (Psalm 5:2a).

- **Morning Devotion Principle #4. Keep reminding yourself to whom you are praying.**

    Heed the sound of my cry for help, my King and my God. For to You I pray (Psalm 5:2a).

- **Morning Devotion Principle #5. Pray in the morning when you need it most.**

    In the morning, O LORD, You will hear my voice (Psalm 5:3a).

- **Morning Devotion Principle #6. Organize your morning prayer-time.**

    In the morning I will order my prayer to You . . . (Psalm 5:3b).

- **Morning Devotion Principle #7. Wait expectantly for God's answers.**

    . . . and eagerly watch (Psalm 5:3c).

G = GREET the day with PRAISE

Obviously, drawing near to God every morning doesn't just happen. It begins with contemplating the majesty and awesome character of God. That's why, even before reading my Bible, I like to sit in the morning, look out a window, read a Psalm or just recite some of His attributes.

One of the things that helps get my "morning praise brain" started is to do what I call Alphabetical Worship. I recite the things I love about God that begin with each letter of the alphabet. For example:

> A: "I thank you, God, that You are ALMIGHTY. You are ALWAYS with me."
>
> B: "I praise you, Jesus, for Your BEAUTY...for BEING my friend."
>
> C: "I am cheering the fact that You, Lord, are the CREATOR who is in CONTROL of my life."

I even recite Scripture:

> E. "EVERY day I will bless You . . ." (Psalm 145:2).
>
> G. "GREAT is the LORD and GREATLY to be praised" (Psalm 96:4).
>
> K. "For the LORD is a great God and a great KING above all gods . . . . " (Psalm 95:3)
>
> R. "REJOICE in the Lord . . ." (Philippians 4:4).

(I have provided in Appendix Four an "Alphabetical Worship Worksheet" to assist you.)

At a camp for High School students, we used Alphabetical Worship to prepare our hearts for communion. We got to the letter X and one teenager shouted out, "Thank you God for xylophones." We all laughed and yes, we gave thanks to God for musical instruments with which we can praise Him, including our voices. Another young woman stood and said, "Thank you, Lord, for your X-ray vision in my life." Now that was an insight for which we all can praise God.

Sitting next to her was a young man wearing a football jacket. He stood and exclaimed with great enthusiasm, "Thank you, God, that you are X-cellent." Okay, so his spelling was wanting, but I would like to believe his heart was right. It is certainly true that our God is excellent.

Then there are those times when I rush off to an early morning appointment or an airport. Although I often use Alphabetical Worship as a praise-guide, I also let the road signs preach to my waking heart: Caution! Green Light! One Way! Red Light! Right Turn Only! Stay to the Right! Slow Down! U Turn! Yield!

IN THE IN-BETWEEN TIME

Morning is not the only time to praise God.

> It is good to give thanks to the LORD and to sing praises to Your name, O Most High; to declare Your lovingkindness in the morning and Your faithfulness by night (Psalm 92:1-2).

> From the rising of the sun to its setting the name of the LORD is to be praised (Psalm 113:3).

G = GREET the day with PRAISE

I especially love the simple words of Psalm 119:

Seven times a day I praise You (Psalm 119:164).

My mind rushes to a special memory of a dear old friend, John Fischer, singing a song he wrote when we were both starting in the ministry. It is called the *All Day Song*. Perhaps you remember the words:

> *Love Him in the morning,*
> *When you see the sun arising.*
> *Love Him in the evening,*
> *'Cause He took you through the day.*
> *And in the in-between-time,*
> *When you feel the pressure coming,*
> *Remember that He loves you,*
> *And He promises to stay.*

I want to challenge you to do the following: For one week set an alarm of some sort for seven times a day (e.g. 8 a.m., 10 a.m., 12 noon, 2 p.m., 4 p.m., 6 p.m., and 8 p.m.). When the alarm goes off take at least one minute to praise God for who He is and what He has done. Recite a verse, sing a song or simply tell Him you love Him. May each minute reflect a heart of worship that declares, "Lord, you are on my mind all day—in the morning, in the evening, and in the in-between-time."

THE DAILY JOY-STEALERS

Sometimes we wake up in a foul mood, knowing fully well these bad attitudes are the very real disabilities that cripple us throughout the day. In order to greet the day with genuine praise, we must deal with the things that stifle our worship, even before the sun rises.

Joy-Stealer #1
"I don't have enough time to do all I need to do today."

Martin Luther is known to have said, "I have so much to do that I shall spend the first three hours in prayer." Quotes like this can either motivate us or intimidate us. Frankly, when I read this I really want to cry out, "Martin, you didn't live in the 21st century." Then again, I remember he had to travel by horseback!

Most of our lives are lived in a flurry of activity where daily expectations far exceed realities. We can relate to the words of Psalm 94:19 as our anxious thoughts "multiply within." We cry out, "If only I had more hours in the day. Twenty-four hours just doesn't seem enough."

Well, I have some bad news. Technically-speaking, it takes the earth twenty-three hours, fifty-six minutes and just over four seconds to spin 360 degrees on its axis. That means the days are shorter than we thought!

Almighty God created our planet as a spinning speck of dust in a cathedral of countless galaxies, each filled with billions of stars. He caused our earth to travel 60,000 miles an hour in an orbit around our sun. He tilted it on an axis at just the right angle to sustain life at twenty-three and a half degrees and set it into a spin of about 1,000 miles per hour. He then created this world with just shy of a twenty-four-hour day and "saw that it was good" (Genesis 1:18). Take to heart the words of Psalm 24:

> The earth is the LORD's and *all* it contains (i.e. including our time) (Psalm 24:1, my addition).

G = GREET the day with PRAISE

As busy as we may think we are, we have enough time to do everything Almighty God wants us to do today. In the frantic hustle and non-stop bustle of our noisy lives this side of Heaven, it takes a lifetime to learn to face the intensity of our days, living out the familiar challenge of Psalm 46:10:

> Be still and know that I am God (Psalm 46:10, King James Version).

Be still. The Hebrew phrase used here is the picturesque word *raphah*. It presents the imagery of us relaxing (maybe with a cup of coffee), sinking down (perhaps in an easy chair), and withdrawing from a battle (of all shapes and sizes, hopefully).

This popular verse continues with the challenge to *know* God. Again, the Hebrew word *yada* is quite beautiful, especially as it speaks about the intimacy with God that comes when we seek Him in those moments of stillness, even in the busiest of times.

Joy-Stealer #2
"I am holding on to frustrations and hurts from yesterday or the days before."

I am convicted by the words of an anonymous poem:

> *I got up early one morning,*
> *And rushed right into the day.*
> *I had so much to accomplish,*
> *I didn't have time to pray.*
> *Troubles just tumbled about me,*
> *And heavier came each task.*
> *Why doesn't God help me, I wondered.*
> *He answered, "You didn't ask."*

The apostle Paul presents a life-altering principle for us to not let a day end with our hearts bombarded with disappointment, anger and bitterness:

> Be angry, and yet do not sin; do not let the sun go down on your anger, and do not give the devil an opportunity (Ephesians 4:26-27).

He is telling us to handle our frustrated expectations and our hurts *today* and not carry into *tomorrow* the unresolved conflicts of *yesterday*. It truly gives the devil an opportunity—a foothold—in our lives and frankly, in the generations to follow. In his epistle to the Romans, Paul adds:

> Be at peace with all men when it is in your power to do it (Romans 12:18).

> So then we pursue the things which make for peace and the building up of one another (Romans 14:19).

We must refuse to store up those costly emotional memories:

> When my anxious thoughts multiply within me,
> Your consolations delight my soul
> (Psalm 94:19).

In Appendix Five I have provided a "Worksheet for Resolving Conflict." I have found it to be a helpful tool to bring the peace we need. It asks us to think through how we, and the person with whom we are in conflict, have violated the "one another" passages in the Bible. Let us consider some of these:

G = GREET the day with PRAISE

- Confess your faults to one another (James 5:16).

- Forgive one another
(Colossians 3:13; Ephesians 4:32).

- Regard one another as more important than yourself
(Philippians 2:3).

- Restore one another (Galatians 6:1).

- Love (self-sacrifice for) one another
(Romans 12:9-10; 1 Peter 4:8; John 13:34; 15:12-17).

- Pray for one another (James 5:16).

- Be kind to one another (Ephesians 4:32).

- Be tenderhearted toward one another
(Ephesians 4:32).

- Don't bite and devour one another (Galatians 5:15).

- Don't provoke one another (Galatians 5:26).

- Don't hate one another (Titus 3:3).

- Don't speak evil against one another (James 4:11).

- Don't judge one another
(Matthew 7:1; Romans 14:13).

Oh, how our *tomorrows* would be so much better if we did these *today*!

Joy-Stealer #3:
"This is going to be a horrible day."

There are some mornings when many of us enter the day filled with such anxiety and intensity, thinking even in those wee hours, we have lost control of our day. We are ready to "power through" without the Real Power we need. We are filled with fear over things that may never happen. Some of us have become obsessed with "awfulizing" and "catastrophizing." Too many are addicted to the chaos of worry. We need to admit the morning pessimism that can ruin our day even before it unfolds. Daily, we must open our hearts to a few attitude-changing passages:

> O LORD . . . please grant me success *today* . . . (Genesis 24:12).
>
> See, I have set before you *today* life and prosperity . . . (Deuteronomy 30:15).
>
> O LORD, I beseech You, may Your ear be attentive to the prayer of Your servant and the prayer of Your servants who delight to revere Your name, and make Your servant successful *today* . . . (Nehemiah 1:11).
>
> Dedicate yourselves *today* to the LORD . . . in order that He may bestow a blessing upon you *today* (Exodus 32:29).

If we dedicate ourselves in the morning to do His will today, we can expect God to bless us. We can cheer the day ahead of us because our Sovereign God is in charge of every one of those 86,400 seconds.

WHAT ABOUT DAILY BIBLE STUDY?

I trust you know the importance of Bible reading and thorough study in which we strive to please God as diligent workers who are "accurately handling the word of truth" (2 Timothy 2:15). I agree with Martin Luther when he made this simple declaration: "Whoever wants to hear God speak should read holy scripture." I am also intrigued by the testimony of people like George Mueller who wrote, "I have read the Bible through one hundred times, and always with increasing delight."

Both of these men of faith are bearing personal testimony of the impact of daily time in the Word of God. Take a moment to mull over the words of Psalm 19 regarding the value of Scripture in our everyday lives:

> The law of the LORD is perfect, restoring the soul. The testimony of the LORD is sure, making wise the simple. The precepts of the LORD are right, rejoicing the heart. The commandment of the LORD is pure, enlightening the eyes. The fear of the LORD is clean, enduring forever. The judgments of the LORD are true; they are righteous altogether. They are more desirable than gold, yes, than much fine gold; sweeter also than honey and the drippings of the honeycomb. Moreover, by them Your servant is warned. In keeping them there is great reward (Psalm 19:7-11).

I refer you to Appendix Six entitled, "God Has Spoken in His Marvelous Word (An Overview of Psalm 19:7-14)" for a more detailed exposition of this amazing passage. It is well worth the time spent.

I fear too many of us rush into our Bible reading without being properly prepared in heart and mind. It can easily become mechanical and meaningless if it is not preceded with prayer and praise. We neglect the flame of desire that must come from our hearts before we even open our Bibles:

> Open my eyes (i.e. the eyes of my heart) that I may behold wonderful things from Your Law (Psalm 119:18, my addition).

In 2015, I published, *"Mastering the Scriptures: A Self Study Course in Effective Bible Study."* It presents one of the pre-requisites to meaningful Bible study—i.e. to begin with P.R.A.Y.E.R:

> P = Praising God for who He is and what He has done in my life.
>
> R = Repenting and asking God to forgive me of my sin.
>
> A = Asking God to use my time of study for His glory.
>
> Y = Yielding my will to Him in a spirit of humility and obedience.
>
> E = Entreating for others who will benefit from my study.
>
> R = Rejoicing in what God will accomplish even before it happens.

G = GREET the day with PRAISE

Let me repeat what I have said many times to my congregation. The longest journey in the world is eighteen inches from our heads to our hearts. Persevering prayer and continual praise are the foundations upon which effective Bible reading and accurate Bible study are built. In order to keep my time in the Word from being lifeless and academic, I often recite the words I saw on a sign on a wall of a church:

P.U.S.H. = Pray Until Something Happens

TODAY'S ASSIGNMENTS

1. Practice using the "Alphabetical Worship Worksheet" in Appendix Four.

2. Following the example in Psalm 119:164, for one week set an alarm of some sort for seven times a day. For example: 8 a.m., 10 a.m., 12 noon, 2 p.m., 4 p.m., 6 p.m., and 8 p.m. When the alarm goes off take just one minute to praise God for who He is and what He has done.

3. What are some of the joy-stealers in your life?

4. What is the relationship of praise to effective Bible study?

5. Read Appendix Seven: "Principles for Effective P.R.A.Y.E.R." Memorize the statements from the Lord's Prayer related to Praising, Repenting, Asking, Yielding, Entreating, Rejoicing).

TOMORROW'S OPPORTUNITIES

1. Read Appendix Six: "God Has Spoken in His Marvelous Word (An Overview of Psalm 19:7-14)."

2. Read Appendix Eight: "Roadblocks to an Effective Prayer-Life."

3. Practice using Appendix Nine: "Daily Bible Reading Ideas."

4. Practice using Appendix Ten: "A Pocket Guide to Effective Bible Study."

CHAPTER TWO

R = REPORT to the day with PURPOSE

One of my life verses encapsulates the entire life of King David in one profound eulogy:

> For David, after he had served the purpose of God in his own generation, fell asleep, and was laid among his fathers . . . (Acts 13:36).

In other words, God had *numbered* David's days (cf. Psalm 90:12) and David filled those days with accomplishing the will of God *in his generation*. What is a generation? Among theologians and Bible scholars, there is much debate. I repeat what I said in the introduction. A generation is a bunch of days lived out *unum diem ad tempus*—one day at a time. King David fulfilled the purpose of God in his own generation, day by day. Oh, how I pray that will be said of me when I die. However, I realize it won't happen automatically.

We are warned in both the Old and New Testament of a wasted life, full of days lived under the bondage of the fool-hearted mantra:

> Let us eat and drink, for tomorrow we may die (Isaiah 22:13).

> Soul, you have many goods laid up for many years to come; take your ease, eat, drink and be merry (Luke 12:19).

If we are going to live a truly successful life as God defines it, we need to report to Him every morning with a great sense of our divine purpose, knowing who we are and why the Lord gave us another day to live. Let me suggest a few reminders that have helped me greatly:

REHEARSING MY DAILY PURPOSE

Daily Reminder #1
"I am a Beloved Child of God. Today, I will not lose focus on who I am and what I am called to do."

The older I get the more my first thought of the day is, "Thank You, Lord, that I am still breathing." It brings new meaning to the last verse of the last psalm:

> Let everything that has breath praise the LORD (Psalm 150:6).

When I wake up with the aches and pains that come with aging, I suppose I should cry out with King David:

> All my bones will say, "LORD, who is like You . . . ?" (Psalm 35:10).

However, I also recognize it is not enough to just enjoy the biological beginning of a day. Our lives in Christ are far more than physical. As children of God, we have new and abundant spiritual lives. That knowledge should dramatically change our perspective every day. I remind us of some Bible passages to rehearse:

R = REPORT to the day with PURPOSE

I [Jesus] came that they may have life and have it abundantly (John 10:10).

But as many as received Him, to them He gave the right to become children of God, even to those who believe in His name, who were born not of blood, nor of the will of the flesh, nor of the will of man, but of God (John 1:12-13).

Therefore, if any man is in Christ, he is a new creature; the old things passed away; behold, new things have come (2 Corinthians 5:17).

If then you have been raised up with Christ, keep seeking the things above, where Christ is, seated at the right hand of God. Set your mind on the things above, not on the things that are on earth. For you have died and your life is hidden with Christ in God. When Christ, who is our life, is revealed, then you also will be revealed with Him in glory (Colossians 3:1-5).

Beloved, now we are children of God . . . (1 John 3:2).

Back in 1971, when I became a born-again follower of Jesus Christ, I listened often to a daily radio broadcast entitled, *"Thru the Bible"* taught by Dr. J. Vernon McGee. At the end of every message he signed off his program with the words, "May God richly bless you, my beloved." What a curious benediction? Yet, I came to learn how amazing it really is to be the *agapetos tou theou*—"The beloved of God."

A few years later, when I became a preacher, I began my Sunday messages with a welcoming, "Good morning, Beloved." It became so familiar that one day I failed to say it and a lady at the door of the church said, "Pastor, you didn't call us 'Beloved.' Don't you love us anymore?"

Daily we must hear the welcoming words of our Heavenly Father to us, His children: "Good morning. You are My beloved child. Act like it today!"

The Scriptures abound in instructions of what is expected of us as the precious children of God. Take a few moments to ponder these clear mandates for our lives. As the beloved children of God, we are daily:

• to not take revenge on others (Romans 12:19).

• to accept being admonished by others
(1 Corinthians 4:14).

• to be steadfast, immovable, always abounding in the work of the Lord (1 Corinthians 15:58).

• to cleanse ourselves from defilement
(2 Corinthians 7:1).

• to be imitators of God (Ephesians 5:1).

• to learn from our beloved fellow bond-servants of Christ (Colossians 1:7).

• to flee from idolatry (like immorality, impurity, passion, evil desire, greed, anger, wrath, malice, slander, abusive speech, and lying (Colossians 3:5, 8-9;
1 Corinthians 10:14).

• to put on a heart of compassion, kindness, humility, gentleness and patience (Colossians 3:12).

R = REPORT to the day with PURPOSE

- to seek to understand what it means to be chosen by God (1 Thessalonians 1:4).

- to thank God for His choice of others (2 Thessalonians 2:13).

- to be quick to hear, slow to speak, and slow to anger (James 1:11).

- to not allow ourselves to be deceived (James 1:16).

- to abstain from fleshly lust (1 Peter 2:11).

- to not be surprised at trials (1 Peter 4:12).

- to be diligent to be found by Him in peace, spotless and blameless (2 Peter 3:14).

- to be on guard against unprincipled people (2 Peter 3:17).

- to test ourselves to see if we are truly in the faith (1 John 4:1).

- to love and serve one another (1 John 4:11; 3 John 1:5).

- to not imitate what is evil but what is good (3 John 1:11).

- to contend earnestly for the faith (Jude 1:3).

- to build ourselves up on our most holy faith (Jude 1:20).

One of the greatest motivations in my life is to take to heart the words our Heavenly Father expressed to Jesus. I believe they are His words for all of us, as His beloved children, when we daily strive to act like His Beloved Son:

> . . . behold, a voice out of the heavens said, "This is My beloved Son, *in whom I am well-pleased*"(Matthew 3:17).

Today, I call us to enter the day enjoying the breadth of what it means to be a beloved child of God and choosing to act accordingly.

Daily Reminder #2
"I am a Soldier of the Cross. Today, I will not let myself get distracted from my duty to my Commander."

I am a Vietnam War veteran, having served on the attack aircraft carrier, USS Kitty Hawk. I recall one day on board when a fellow sailor was not paying attention during flight operations and he was blown off the flight deck by one of the jet engines. Whatever distracted him cost him his life. His name is permanently etched on a memorial wall in Washington, D.C.

As born-again believers, we are full-time Soldiers of the Cross, not weekend warriors on temporary duty. We are always doing battle against the flesh, the devil and the world's twisted values. Therefore, we must not let ourselves get distracted or entangled. So said the apostle Paul, our fellow soldier:

> Suffer hardship with me, as a good soldier of Christ Jesus. No soldier in active service

R = REPORT to the day with PURPOSE

entangles himself in the affairs of everyday life, so that he may please the one who enlisted him as a soldier (2 Timothy 2:3-4).

What are some of those entanglements? Sometimes they are really important things like family, friends, ministry, work, and studies. However, even these good things can keep us from doing our best thing—fulfilling the purpose of God in our own generation. Simply stated: First things first—Him!

For a number of years, there has been circulated around churches a declaration that expresses this well. Unfortunately, we do not know the author and it has most likely changed from the original version. It is entitled, *"I Am a Soldier."* May it encourage our hearts today:

> <u>I am a soldier</u> in the Army of God. The Lord Jesus Christ is my commanding officer. The Holy Bible is my code of conduct. Faith, prayer and the Word are my weapons of warfare. I have been taught the Word of God, trained by experience, tried by adversity and tested by fire. I am a volunteer in this army, and I am enlisted for eternity. I will retire in this army at time's end or die in this army; but I will not sell out, be talked out or pushed out.
>
> I am faithful, reliable, capable, and dependable. If my God needs me, I am there. If he needs me in Sunday school, to teach children, work with youth, help adults or just sit and learn, he can use me, because I am there. <u>I am a soldier</u>. I do not need to be pampered, petted, primed up, picked up or pepped up. <u>I am a soldier</u>.

HAVE A G.R.E.A.T. DAY

I am not a wimp. I am in place, saluting my King, obeying his orders, praising his name and building his kingdom. No one has to send me flowers, gifts, food, cards, candy, or give me handouts. I do not need to be cuddled, cradled, cared for or catered to. I am committed.

I cannot have my feelings hurt bad enough to turn me around. I cannot be discouraged enough to turn me aside. I cannot lose enough to cause me to quit. When Jesus called me into his army, I had nothing. If I end up with nothing, I will still break even. I will win. My God will supply all my needs. I am more than a conqueror. I will always triumph. I can do all things through Christ.

Demons cannot defeat me. People cannot disillusion me. Weather cannot weary me. Sickness cannot stop me. Battles cannot beat me. Money cannot buy me. Governments cannot silence me and hell cannot handle me. <u>I am a soldier</u>.

Even death cannot destroy me, for when my commander calls me from this battlefield, he will promote me to live with him. <u>I am a soldier</u>, and I'm marching, claiming victory! I will not give up. <u>I am a soldier</u>! I will not turn around. I am a soldier marching heaven bound! Here I stand. Will you stand with me? (Author Unknown)

Today, I ask us to stand with our fellow Soldiers of the Cross and salute the Lord Jesus Christ as our Commanding Officer, the King of Kings and Lord of Lords.

R = REPORT to the day with PURPOSE

Daily Reminder #3
   "I am a Servant of God. Today, I will obey my Master at all costs."

In one of my very first public messages as a new pastor I developed an outline that was stimulated by a season of doubt when I was asking myself, "How can I be sure I know the Lord?" A simple outline has become a life message for the half century of my teaching ministry:

   I.   To know Him is to love Him.
   II. To love Him is to obey Him.
   III. To obey Him is to serve Him.

It has been well said that we are slaves of God and servants of men. By definition, faithful servants are known for their willingness to obey their masters unconditionally. We must enter the day with an attitude that says, "No matter what comes my way, I exist to do the bidding of my Lord today." Doing so puts us in good company with Mary, the mother of Jesus (Luke 1:38), James (James 1:1), Paul (Romans 1:1), Peter (2 Peter 1:1), and Jude (Jude 1:1). All of them humbly called themselves a "bond-servant" of the Lord.

I am sure many of us have watched the movie, *Ben Hur*. Graphically depicted are the scenes of slaves who were the "under-rowers" on the lowest level of a Roman warship. They were, quite literally, chained to the oars and to one another.

The New Testament Greek word for "under-rowing slave" (*huperetes*) is primarily used to describe those who are "chained to their responsibilities," regardless of whether they are the lowest slaves or the highest officials. In Acts 26:16, the word is used of the apostle Paul's calling as a minister and a gospel witness.

In 1 Corinthians 4:1 the apostle Paul uses the same word to speak of all believers as "ministers" of Christ who are "joined" to Him (cf. Romans 7:4). It reminds me of the similar words spoken by Moses to the Children of Israel:

> . . . you shall serve Him and cling ("cleave, stick," Hebrew: *dabak*) to Him (Deuteronomy 10:12).

We are stuck to our Lord, shackled to our calling and chained to one another as slaves of God and servants of men. As such we are called to be servant-spouses, servant-parents, servant-workers, servant-ministers and servant-witnesses of the Gospel to our world.

With that special commission comes great servant-opportunities every day. Once again, we point to the popular declaration of Joshua:

> . . . choose for yourselves *today* whom you will serve . . . as for me and my house, we will serve the LORD (Joshua 24:15).

This could also mean we may be chained to a special calling to be servant-sufferers, just as the apostle Paul was:

> . . . pray on my behalf, that utterance may be given to me in the opening of my mouth, to make known with boldness the mystery of the gospel, for which I am an ambassador in chains; that in proclaiming it I may speak boldly, as I ought to speak" (Ephesians 6:19-20).

R = REPORT to the day with PURPOSE

I am reminded of the poignant words of Alfred Lord Tennyson in his narrative poem, *The Charge of the Light Brigade*:

> *Theirs not to make reply.*
> *Theirs not to reason why.*
> *Theirs but to do and die.*
> *Into the valley of Death.*
> *Rode the six hundred.*

Today, I call on the countless number of true disciples to rise and declare to our Heavenly Father that we are cleaved to Him, joined to Christ, united with each other and chained to our calling and responsibilities. Let's tell Him we are willing to serve Him today "with gladness," no matter what the sacrifice (cf. Psalm 100:2; Colossians 3:24).

Daily Reminder #4
"I am an Ambassador of Jesus Christ. Today, I will represent my King in everything I say and do."

When I was thirty years old, I took my first overseas ministry trip throughout India. I will never forget the sights and sounds (and even the smells) of that incredibly foreign country. Towards the end of our month-long trip, we walked into the American Embassy in New Delhi, the Indian capital. There, my senses were filled with reminders of home: an American flag, American Marines, American music, American art and, although it may have been my famished imagination, I could even smell American hamburgers and fries! All thirty of us grateful pastors sang "God Bless America" in the echoing rotunda of the beautiful, American-style building. What a memorable experience! Since that day I have thought often about that welcome taste of home in a foreign land.

As one who has trusted in Jesus Christ alone for his salvation, I do not consider this world my home. The Bible is clear that, as born-again Christians, we are aliens and strangers in this foreign land. Our true citizenship is in Heaven (1 Peter 2:11; Ephesians 2:19; Philippians 3:20-21). Therefore, our primary allegiance is to the King of Kings, under whom we serve as emissaries. The apostle Paul reminds us of our unique calling:

> Therefore, we are ambassadors for Christ, as though God were entreating through us; we beg you on behalf of Christ, be reconciled to God (2 Corinthians 5:20).

As ambassadors of Jesus Christ, our job description is to live in this foreign land, Earth, as representatives of our home country, Heaven. Although our heavenly citizenship comes with tremendous privileges, it is also expected that we personally live in such a way that reflects the values of the King we represent. Furthermore, each Christian family and local church is to be an Embassy of Heaven, where those godly virtues exist and are readily seen by all men, so they will glorify our Father in Heaven (Matthew 5:16).

Today, I call us to choose to live our lives at home, at work (or school) and in the community, as ambassadors of Christ, giving those around us a taste of Heaven's values in this foreign land.

R = REPORT to the day with PURPOSE

Daily Reminder #5:
"I am a Messenger of the Gospel. Today, I will join with others in praying and participating in sharing the good news with the world."

The good news of the gospel is that we are saved by grace alone (*sola gratia*), through faith alone (*sola fide*), in Christ alone (*solus Christus*), because that is what the Scriptures alone teach (*sola Scriptura*), and what brings the greatest glory to God alone (*soli deo gloria*). I remind us of a couple of key verses:

> For by grace you have been saved through faith; and that not of yourselves, it is the gift of God; not as a result of works, so that no one may boast (Ephesians 2:8-9).

> He saved us, not on the basis of deeds which we have done in righteousness, but according to His mercy, by the washing of regeneration and renewing by the Holy Spirit (Titus 3:5).

Since salvation is solely the work of God in people's lives, we must daily be on the lookout for those who the Holy Spirit has prepared to come to a saving knowledge of the Lord Jesus Christ. This can be done a number of ways:

First, I keep in my Bible a list of prayer items, including the names of my immediate and extended family, as well as friends and neighbors. I pray often for them, especially those who I am not sure have a personal relationship to Jesus Christ. Of course, I also pray God would stimulate those family members and friends who do know Him to have an even greater passion to share the good news of the Gospel of Grace.

Secondly, I have made it a morning practice to pray for a different country every day. To remind myself, I have a series of coffee cups with the flags or names of a variety of countries. I also keep on hand a hard copy and the electronic version of the latest version of *"Operation World: The Definitive Prayer Guide to Every Nation."* It provides me valuable information on the spiritual condition of each country.

It is our calling as Messengers of the Gospel to prayerfully broadcast the good news with family, friends, neighbors, co-workers, and fellow citizens of our city, state, nation and world. Every day we can prayerfully take to heart the age-old challenge:

> Proclaim good tidings of His salvation *day to day* (Psalm 96:2).

> And [Jesus] was saying to them, "The harvest is plentiful, but the laborers are few; therefore beseech the Lord of the harvest to send out laborers into His harvest" (Luke 10:2).

Of course, we should not forget the timeless words of the Great Commission. Christ expects us to participate in the spreading of the good news into the outermost parts of the world and equipping people to follow Him as re-producing disciples:

> Go therefore and make disciples of all the nations…and lo, I am with you always, even to the end of the age (Matthew 28:19-20).

R = REPORT to the day with PURPOSE

We must bear in mind this "Lifetime Global Great Commission" is made up of a number of "Daily Local Little Commissions," especially to those whom God places before us. In Appendix Eleven: "My Daily Prayer Journal," you will be asked to list people for whom you will be praying for opportunities to share the gospel soon.

Today, I ask us to cry out to the Lord of the Harvest, asking Him to allow us to actively participate in the Great Commission, one Little Commission at a time. May He open doors as only He can.

Let me summarize. Proverbs 16:4 reminds us that the Lord "has made everything for its own purpose." That includes His calling in our lives. One day at a time, let's strive to fulfill the purpose of God in our generation (cf. Acts 13:36). Begin the day with these reminders:

- "I am a Beloved Child of God. Today, I will not lose focus on who I am and what I am called to do."

- "I am a Soldier of the Cross. Today, I will not let myself get distracted from my duty to my Commander."

- "I am a Servant of God. Today, I will obey my Master at all costs."

- "I am an Ambassador of Jesus Christ. Today, I will represent My King in everything I say and do."

- "I am a Messenger of the Gospel. Today, I will join with others in praying and participating in sharing the good news with the world."

TODAY'S ASSIGNMENTS

1. Report the results from Assignment #2 in Chapter One.

2. Which of the five daily reminders do you need to focus on most today?

3. Practice using Appendix Eleven: "My Daily Prayer Journal."

4. Make a "Top Ten List" of family, friends, and neighbors who need to hear the Gospel. Pray for an open door to share the Good News with them.

TOMORROW'S OPPORTUNITIES

1. Ask for a list of missionaries, mission agencies, and parachurch organizations your church supports. Set aside some time to pray for each one on a regular basis.

2. Pick one day a month where you will pray for your city, state, nation and world.

3. Schedule a regular time to pray for individual countries. You might find it helpful to go to www.operationworld.com and download or secure a printed copy of the latest edition of *"Operation World: The Definitive Prayer Guide to Every Nation."*

4. Make a more extensive list to daily remind yourself of who you are in Christ. For example:
"I am adopted into the family of God."
"I am a forgiven sinner."
"I am a new creation."
"I am a joint heir with Christ."
"I am a citizen of Heaven."
"I am the salt and light of the earth."
"I am a temple of the Holy Spirit."
"I am a chosen child of promise."
"I am a member of Christ's Body, the Church."
"I am _____."

CHAPTER THREE

E = ENGAGE the day with a PLAN

I have not always been a planner. Quite the contrary. Just ask my poor wife who, as my new bride, spent her honeymoon night in a dilapidated, old hotel room in Salinas, California because I failed to make a hotel reservation in Monterey, during the busiest weekend of the year. It didn't take me long to see the value of some forethought.

As the popular saying reminds us: "Failure to plan is a plan to fail." Now, after almost forty-eight years of marriage, I am a planner—an over-planner, some close to me might say. That too can be problematic. Even a seemingly good plan, well laid out but without proper focus, can fail miserably. Just ask Job:

> My days are past, my plans are torn apart, even the wishes of my heart . . . . (Job 17:11).

FOCUS! FOCUS! FOCUS!

I was once an avid target shooter, quite familiar with the need to focus on the front sight, the target and what's behind it. I love the story of the army rifle expert who entered a town to find a number of hand-drawn targets with bullet holes dead center. He could not wait to meet this amazing shooter. The soldier was surprised when the townspeople pointed him to an old man with thick glasses and a beat-up old rifle. He asked how someone like him could shoot so well. The old man replied, "Son, it's quite simple. I shoot first and draw the circle later."

If we are going to have a great day—a successful day in the eyes of the Lord—then we must commit ourselves throughout the day to engage in God's plans and not our own. Commenting on Psalm 37:23, English evangelist George Mueller wrote in his Bible, "The *steps* of a man are ordered by the Lord. So are the *stops*!"

I am so very guilty of making my daily plans, without considering what God wants for me. Pay attention to the words of James, the brother of our Lord:

> Come now, you who say, 'Today or tomorrow, we shall go to such and such a city, and spend a year there and engage in business and make a profit.' Yet you do not know what your life will be like tomorrow. You are just a vapor that appears for a little while and then vanishes away (James 4:13).

Consider also the words of wise King Solomon 3,000 years ago:

> Trust in the LORD with all your heart and do not lean on your own understanding. In all your ways acknowledge Him, and He will make your paths straight. Do not be wise in your own eyes. Fear the LORD and turn away from evil (Proverbs 3:5-7).

> The mind of man plans his way, but the LORD directs his steps (Proverbs 16:9).

> Do not boast about tomorrow, for you do not know what a day may bring forth (Proverbs 27:1).

E = ENGAGE the day with a PLAN

Now, let's add some reminders from the Psalms:

> Make Your way straight before me (Psalm 5:8).
>
> For He is our God, and we are the people of His pasture, and the sheep of His hand. *Today*, if you would hear His voice . . . (Psalm 95:7).

We are to commit our works—our everyday actions—to the Lord who can be trusted with every detail. Even our little steps will be established by the One who has His eye upon us and will guide us every step of the way (cf. Proverbs 16:3). In other words, don't shoot first and draw the circle later. "Ready! Aim! Fire!" is a much more effective daily plan than "Ready! Fire! Aim!"

MY DAILY PRIORITY LIST

"Hi, I'm Jim. I am a Listaholic!" Most of us make lists. However, real list-people like me are those who not only make lists of what they need to do but will even write down the things they did that were not on the list and then mark them off! We even have lists pointing to other lists. Updating them brings such satisfaction. In fact, if we are not careful, making the lists can almost feel like we are getting something done.

Even if you are not a list person and like to be completely spontaneous (I can't even imagine such a life!), I still think it is important for all of us to prayerfully and carefully outline and prioritize our daily tasks. Now, thanks to electronic applications, we have elaborate systems in which we are able to do this easily. However, it still comes down to the basics—formulating a prioritizing grid.

ALWAYS ON THE LIST

The following are things that should always be on our "To Do List" for TODAY:

- Spend at least thirty minutes in prayer, praise and reflection from our personal Bible reading.

- Listen to our favorite sacred music. Recite or sing the words of one of our favorite hymns or spiritual songs.

- Tell at least one person "I love you" and "I'm proud of you" and "I appreciate you."

- Exercise for at least 15-30 minutes (e.g. Walk at least 5,000 to 10,000 steps).

- Eat well. Keep a record.

- Tell one person about Christ.

- Send a word of encouragement to at least three people.

- Greet at least one neighbor and help, where needed.

- Take fifteen minutes for complete silence or take a nap.

- Do at least one project we would rather not do.

- Do at least one thing on our "Get Ahead" (Future Project) List.

E = ENGAGE the day with a PLAN

From here we move on to the rest of our list, sorted by categories (e.g. home, work, school, ministry, calls, future projects, etc.):

A. The things I <u>must</u> do today (A_1 A_2 A_3, etc.)
B. The things I <u>should</u> do today (B_1 B_2 B_3, etc.)
C. The things I <u>would like</u> to do today (C_1 C_2 C_3, etc.)
D. The things I <u>must</u> do in the future (D_1 D_2 D_3, etc.)

(A detailed worksheet is available in Appendix Twelve: "My Daily Priority List.")

By the way, I often reward myself for being diligent with the things I <u>must</u> do and <u>should</u> do by making sure I sprinkle my day with some daily things I <u>would like</u> to do. After all, ice cream is God's gift to Listaholics like me and those "fly by the seat of the pants" people who are happy they are not fanatical list-people.

Not everything on our list can be done on that day; nor should they be. There are always unexpected turns and interruptions. The old saying is quite true that "the plans are man's, but the odds are God's." We must pray through our daily plans with the following heavenly perspectives in mind:

... You number my steps ... (i.e. not just my days) (Job 14:16, my addition).

The counsel of the LORD stands forever, the plans of His heart from generation to generation (Psalm 33:11).

For He is our God, and we are the people of His pasture and the sheep of His hand. *Today* if you would *hear His voice* (Psalm 95:7).

There is a way which seems right to a man but its end is the way of death (Proverbs 16:25).

Many plans are in a man's heart, but the counsel of the LORD will stand (Proverbs 19:21).

For as the heavens are higher than the earth, so are My ways higher than your ways and My thoughts than your thoughts (Isaiah 55:9).

As I review my daily list, I often recite the poignant words of former professional baseball player, Bobby Richardson, who prayed, "Dear God. Your will. Nothing more. Nothing less. Nothing else. Amen."

What about those daily decisions in which you are undecided between two or even three good options? I refer you to Appendix Thirteen: "How Do I Make Biblical Decisions Every Day?" In it you will be asked to answer a number of questions regarding those decisions, especially having to discern what God would have you do. This exercise has protected me many times from "shooting first and drawing the circle later."

DEVELOPING MY LIFE FOCUS

Beyond the daily list of prioritized things to do and identifying the items to be placed in our future project file, comes the important task of developing a plan for our lives.

Appendix Fourteen is a worksheet entitled, "Developing My Life Focus." I designed it for my own long-term personal planning. This exercise will ask you to think about why you exist, and what you desire the final chapters of your life to look like. You will be challenged to create a timeline of God's faithfulness from the time you were born to today, in hopes of reminding you that "he who began a good work in you will perfect it until the day of Christ Jesus" (Philippians 1:6). Recognizing God's amazing work in your life in the past will springboard you into placing your trust and confidence in Him for your future:

> For such is God, our God forever and ever; He will guide us until death (Psalm 48:14).

In order to bring your life into better focus, you will also be given the opportunity to identify your desires and dreams (even the impossible ones), as well as your spiritual gifts, talents, skills, education, hobbies, and ministry-related training and experience. God wants to use all of these to make you into the person He designed you to be.

You will be asked to identify your victories as well as your failures and limitations. These will remind you of God's power and grace in your life in the best and worst of times. You will end this exercise by creating a list of opportunities and the names of those with whom you need to consult in order to take the necessary next steps today and tomorrow—the first days of the rest of your life. Throughout this life-impacting exercise, keep in mind the wonderful promises of God:

> I [God] will instruct you and teach you in the way which you should go; I will counsel you *with My eye upon you* (Psalm 32:8).

The plans of the heart belong to man, but the *answer of the tongue* is from the LORD. All the ways of a man are clean in his own sight, but the LORD weighs the motives. Commit your works to the LORD, and your plans will be established (Proverbs 16:1-3).

The steps of a man are established by the LORD and He delights in his way . . . *the LORD is the One who holds his hand* (Psalm 37:23-24).

Oh, how I thank our Heavenly Father for His eyes watching over us and the answers from His tongue leading us. In the process, He holds our hands as He helps us make our plans step by step, day by day, over a lifetime. *Unum deim ad tempus.*

E = ENGAGE the day with a PLAN

TODAY'S ASSIGNMENTS

1. Let's review:

G = GREET the day with PRAISE.
R = REPORT to the day with PURPOSE.
E = ENGAGE the day with a PLAN.

2. Are you a rigid planner or are you generally more spontaneous? Which do you prefer and why?

3. Practice using Appendix Twelve: "My Daily Priority List."

4. What are some things you would add to your "Must Do" list every day?

TOMORROW'S OPPORTUNITIES

1. Practice using Appendix Thirteen: "How Do I Make Biblical Decisions Every Day?"

2. Set apart some time to complete Appendix Fourteen: "Developing My Life Focus." (Note: You will need a few days to do this assignment.)

3. Ask your spouse, a relative or a friend to do the same assignment and share your answers in a time of discussion and personal planning.

CHAPTER FOUR
A = ANALYZE the day with PERSPECTIVE

"The unexamined life is not worth living."
(Attributed to Socrates)

You have tried my heart; You have visited me by night; You have tested me and found nothing . . . . (Psalm 17:3).

Let us examine and probe our ways, and let us return to the LORD (Lamentations 3:40).

Arise, cry out in the night as the watches of the night begin; pour out your heart in the presence of the LORD . . . . (Lamentations 2:19, New International Version).

My wife and I are so very different in how we approach yardwork. She calls it gardening. To me it is just hard work. After hours of weeding and pruning, I look ahead and groan at what is yet to be done; she looks back and rejoices over what has been completed.

When it comes to the daily practice of "plowing through life," many of us have a tendency to look forward to tomorrow's tasks and rarely look back and celebrate what God allowed us to accomplish today. This can be very unhealthy spiritually and emotionally. Just thinking about the workload ahead can also drain us physically.

In his Gospel, Luke records what happened when the people saw the power of God demonstrated before their eyes. Our worship-arts pastor calls them

"God-sightings" and "God-moments." They can be amazing spiritual vista points, if we just take the time to look.

> . . . they were all struck with astonishment ("ecstasy, wonderment," Greek: *extasis*) and began glorifying God; and they were filled with fear ("reverence, awe, responding to power," Greek: *phobos*), saying, 'We have seen remarkable ("unexpected, incredible, wonderful, uncommon," Greek: *parodoxos*) things *today*' (Luke 5:26).

In my church office I have a ship's bell I call "The Praise Bell." When I first moved in, I encouraged my ministry staff to ring the bell whenever they wanted to have us all join them in praising God for something unexpected He did. Few have done it. (It is quite loud!)

In Micah 7:7 the prophet expresses he will watch expectantly for the Lord. These same words are used of a watchman and remind me of modern-day guards whose instructions are, "Look up. Look down. Look all around."

As our day unfolds, we need to take some time to look all around for the amazing things God did and then "remark about the remarkable." We need to ring the praise bell more. Admittedly, I don't do this enough. I am quick to look ahead to tomorrow and ignore today.

To be more intentional about this, I developed some questions to encourage us to analyze our day from God's perspective. It is best to do these in the early evening. I suggest we let the end of our evening meal or the sunset be our reminder. They can even be discussion points with our loved ones.

A = ANALYZE the day with PERSPECTIVE

QUESTIONS FOR THE END OF THE DAY

End of the Day Question #1
What remarkable thing did I see God do today?

> Behold, the LORD our God has shown us His glory and His greatness, and we have heard His voice from the midst of the fire; we have seen *today* that <u>God speaks with man</u>, yet he lives (Deuteronomy 5:24).

Almighty God has revealed Himself to us throughout the day in a number of truly amazing ways:

- He speaks with us through the evidence of His providential goodness (Matthew 5:45).

- He speaks with us through the leading of His indwelling Holy Spirit (Galatians 5:18; Ephesians 5:18).

- He speaks with us through specific instruction in His Holy Word (2 Timothy 3:16).

- He speaks with us through the fellowship and encouragement of His people (Hebrews 10:24-25).

- He speaks with us through the power of His creation (Psalm 19:1-6).

I am what some might call a "backyard astronomer." I love to point out to any who will listen just how powerful and awesome our Creator is. During my "star-talks" I love to share about worship as "wow-ship."

What truly amazing way did God reveal Himself to us today? What were the evidences of His goodness, His leading, His instruction, the fellowship of His people, and the power of His creation? In what way did He "wow" us? Tell yourself! Tell Him! Tell others!

End of the Day Question #2
  In what ways was today successful as God has defined success?

It has been well said that a pat on the back and a kick in the behind are not far from each other anatomically, but there is a world of difference in terms of their impact. It has also been observed that applause is simply a pat on the back from a distance.

Perhaps we grew up rarely hearing someone say they are proud of us. Yet, there are most likely some things we did today that were truly worthy of praise. So, let's go right ahead and give ourselves a few pats on the back. And listen carefully. We might just hear Heaven's applause!

While we are at it, we might let this be a reminder to also pat someone else on the back—someone who, like us, is worthy of mercy. I love the story of the father who was trying to be positive when his teenager's report card had all failing grades. "Well, son, at least I know you weren't cheating!"

End of the Day Question #3.
  In what areas would God say I did poorly today?

Search me, O God, and know my heart. Try me ("scrutinize, test like gold," Hebrew: *bachan*) and know my anxious thoughts. And see if there be any hurtful ("painful, idolatrous,

A = ANALYZE the day with PERSPECTIVE

sorrow-producing," Hebrew: *'otseb*) way in me; and lead me in the everlasting way (Psalm 139:23-24).

I often say to my pastoral and ministry staff that failures are not always fatal, if we learn from them. In fact, on many levels, failure can be a backdoor to success. At the end of the day, let's think about the things that did not go well today from God's perspective—even those times when we were not listening to the Lord and we knew it. Refuse to let it become a habit:

> *Today* if you hear His voice, do not harden your hearts . . . (Hebrews 3:15).

We do well to rehearse the honest testimony of 2 Samuel 3:39: "I am weak today."—i.e. "Lord, I blew it today." We also need to follow the painful counsel of King Saul as he realized God was not answering His prayers:

> Draw near here . . . and *investigate* and see how this sin has happened today" (1 Samuel 14:38).

The Christian life often takes a few steps backwards (cf. Jeremiah 7:24). Admit it! Confess it! Turn from it! Move forward! Tomorrow is another day! Hold on to the hope presented in Psalm 30:5, even when we know we have grieved the Holy Spirit of God (cf. Ephesians 4:30):

> For His anger is but for a moment. His favor is for a lifetime. Weeping may last for the night, but a shout of joy comes in the morning (Psalm 30:5).

End of the Day Question #4
What would God have me do better tomorrow?

Our Heavenly Father is the Lord of Mercy and the God of Second Chances. That should be a great attitude-changer. I love the possibility of tomorrow.

> Therefore, do not be anxious for tomorrow; for tomorrow will care for itself. Each day has enough trouble of its own (Matthew 6:34).

I am moved by what God said to King Jehoshaphat when he was surrounded by armies to the north, south and east and had his back to the Mediterranean Sea to the west.

> Tomorrow go down against them . . . . (i.e. Go to bed, Jehoshaphat!). You need not fight in this battle; station yourselves, stand and see the salvation of the LORD on your behalf, O Judah and Jerusalem. Do not fear or be dismayed; tomorrow go out to face them, for *the LORD is with you.*"(2 Chronicles 20:16-17, my addition).

Did you catch those timely words? *"For the LORD is with you."* These are similar to words spoken to Moses in Exodus 4, Gideon in Judges 6, Jeremiah in Jeremiah 1, Jonah in Jonah 4 and Jesus' fearful disciples in Matthew 28. Thus, we can look to Heaven and say: "Thank you, Lord, that tomorrow is another day. We will endeavor, by Your help, to do better." We will make it our daily challenge to, in the words of the apostle Paul, "excel still more" (1 Thessalonians 4:1, 10).

A = ANALYZE the day with PERSPECTIVE

Our next chapter reminds us to end the day as we began it . . . with prayer and praise!

It is good to give thanks to the LORD and to sing praise to Your name, O Most High; to declare Your lovingkindness *in the morning and Your faithfulness by night* (Psalm 92:1-2).

TODAY'S ASSIGNMENTS

1. Let's review:

G = GREET the day with PRAISE.
R = REPORT to the day with PURPOSE.
E = ENGAGE the day with a PLAN.
A = ANALYZE the day with PERSPECTIVE.

Note: If you are doing this assignment well before the end of the day, consider yesterday as you go through the following questions.

2. What remarkable thing did you see God do today?

3. In what ways was today successful as God has defined success?

4. In what areas would God say you did poorly today?

5. What would God have you do better tomorrow?

TOMORROW'S OPPORTUNITIES

1. Practice using Appendix Fifteen: "My Daily Accountability Worksheet."

2. If this is a season of sin and rebellion, reflect on Appendix Sixteen: "The A.C.T.S. of Repentance."

CHAPTER FIVE

T = TERMINATE the day with PRAYER

> "Prayer should be the key of the day and the lock of the night. Devotion should be both the morning star and the evening star."
> (C.H. Spurgeon)

> ... His song will be with me in the night, a prayer to the God of my life (Psalm 42:8).

> My eyes anticipate the night watches, that I may meditate on Your word (Psalm 119:148).

In the Hebrew culture a new day begins the evening before (e.g. "evening and morning, the first day" cf. Genesis 1:5, etc.). In the Hebrew mindset, the day starts with evening worship, not with the morning wake up.

Before we go to bed, we can emulate the evening prayers of some of the great men of old, understanding these were really prayers for the <u>beginning</u> of their day.

THE EVENING PRAYER OF NEHEMIAH

> ... let Your ear now be attentive and Your eyes open to hear the prayer of Your servant which I am praying before You now, day *and night* ... O LORD, I beseech You, may Your ear be attentive to the prayer of Your servant and the prayer of Your servants who delight to revere Your name, and make Your servant successful *today* ... (Nehemiah 1:6, 11).

THE EVENING PRAYER OF ELIJAH

At *the time of the offering of the evening sacrifice,* Elijah the prophet came near and said, "O LORD, the God of Abraham, Isaac and Israel, *today* let it be known that You are God in Israel, and that I am Your servant, and that I have done all these things at Your word" (1 Kings 18:36).

I grew up at a time when parents taught their children to recite a nightly prayer that was, in my young mind, one of the most terrifying prayers ever written:

Now I lay me down to sleep.
I pray the Lord my soul to keep.
If I should die before I wake,
I pray the Lord my soul to take.

I remember clearly at the age of nine refusing to go to sleep, thinking I might die if I did. I much prefer the evening prayers of Nehemiah, David and Elijah.

DEALING WITH THOSE NIGHTLY DISTRACTIONS

Nicholas of Flue was a Swiss hero who forestalled a civil war in his country. He was later recognized as the patron saint of Switzerland. His prayer speaks to my heart:

"O Lord, take from me what keeps me from Thee; give me what brings me to Thee; and take myself and give me Thyself" (Nicholas of Flue).

T = TERMINATE the day with PRAYER

We live in a noisy world. Traffic. Sirens. Crying children. Bickering teens. Some of it is our fault. Like many of you, I am guilty of letting the noise of the T.V. put me to sleep. Too many nights I have fallen asleep scanning the news, emails and texts. We have let electronic noise invade the valuable silence the night can offer. Ecclesiastes 3:7 speaks of "a time to be silent."

Then, there is the emotional noise—the things that shout in our brains, especially at night. Worry. Fear. Anxiety. Anger. Bitterness. Frustration. We need to learn to live out the command of Ephesians 4:26 and not let the sun set on all of those. Many of us can easily relate to David's description of his conflicted heart:

> ... I am restless in my complaint (Hebrew: *ruwd*) and am surely distracted (Hebrew: *huwm*) (Psalm 55:2).

The Hebrew words *ruwd* and *huwm* used here really strike home. Putting both descriptive words together, David is crying out in the night, "I am restless, agitated and can't be still. I am so distracted. My life is noisy and in an uproar. In fact, it feels like it has been thrown into utter confusion."

As challenging as it is to be quiet in a noisy world, even of our own making, we would do well to follow the practice of the psalmists:

> My soul *waits in silence* for God only ...
> (Psalm 62:1, 5).

> Surely I have composed and *quieted* my soul,
> like a weaned child rests against his mother. My soul is like a weaned child within me
> (Psalm 131:2).

> ...meditate in your heart upon your bed and *be still*. Selah (Psalm 4:4).

The Hebrew word translated "wait in silence" in Psalm 62:5 and "quieted" in Psalm 131:2, as well as the phrase "be still" in Psalm 4:4 are all translations of the same Hebrew word: *damam*. Simply put, it means to stop the noise. Additionally, the word *selah* at the end of Psalm 4:4 and many other psalms is believed to be a musical notation, asking us to pause. I see these as God's reminders to stop and do some serious thinking about the things that matter to God.

May the Lord stir our hearts to seek out those nightly *Selah Moments*. It may even mean we have to get up at midnight for some quiet time to "pause and ponder."

> At midnight I shall rise to give thanks to You because of your righteous ordinances (Psalm 119:62).

There continues to be a huge debate as to whether midnight belongs to today or tomorrow. Okay, let's get up at 11:59 p.m. and be done with the banter. Even those sleepy moments can be precious times of praise and adoration. And, think about it. At midnight or 12:01 a.m. (if we insist) we have truly TERMINATED the day with PRAYER and GREETED the day with PRAISE. Now, that's what I call efficiency! Once again, we rehearse the first two verses of Psalm 92:

> It is good to give thanks to the LORD and to sing praise to Your name, O Most High; to declare Your lovingkindness *in the morning and Your faithfulness by night* (Psalm 92:1-2).

T = TERMINATE the day with PRAYER

Now we can sleep, with the peace-producing promises of the Word of God running through our minds:

> I lay down and slept. I awoke, for the LORD sustains me. I will not be afraid. I will not be afraid of ten thousands of people who have set themselves against me round about
> (Psalm 3:5-6).
>
> The fear of the LORD leads to life, so that one may sleep satisfied, untouched by evil
> (Proverbs 19:23).
>
> When you lie down, you will not be afraid; when you lie down, your sleep will be sweet
> (Proverbs 3:24).

Based on these promises and others, permit me my own personal re-write of that old childhood prayer:

> *Now I lay me down to sleep.*
> *I pray the Lord my soul to keep.*
> *Give me the peace to make me still,*
> *That I may wake to do Your will.*

TODAY'S ASSIGNMENTS

1. Let's review:

G = GREET the day with PRAISE.
R = REPORT to the day with PURPOSE.
E = ENGAGE the day with a PLAN.
A = ANALYZE the day with PERSPECTIVE.
T = TERMINATE the day with PRAYER.

2. What are the distractions to being "quiet before the Lord?" List the practical things you can do to keep the "noise" down.

3. For one week, turn off all electronic devices at least thirty minutes before going to sleep. Let this be your "time to be silent" (Ecclesiastes 3:7). Ask God for some "Selah Moments." Describe them below:

TOMORROW'S OPPORTUNITIES

1. Read King David's evening prayer in Psalm 141:1-9, underlining those portions that especially speak to your heart:

2. Review all of the verses in Chapter Five and decide on two you will work on memorizing. Write them below:

a.

b.

CONCLUSION

(The Beginning of the Journey Towards the Best Days of Our Lives)

"CARPE DIEM: SEIZE THE DAY"

You may have heard this expression from the ancient Latin poem by Horace, the Roman poet, writing around 50 BC. The actual quote, translated into English, goes something like this:

> "Carpe diem! Rejoice while you are alive. Enjoy the day. Live life to the fullest. Make the most of what you have. It is later than you think." (Quintus Horatius Flaccus, aka: Horace)

A hundred years after Horace, the apostle Paul said something similar:

> Conduct yourselves with wisdom toward outsiders, *making the most of the opportunity* (Colossians 4:5).

There are few sins in my life more heart-hardening than letting myself become a victim of the day, rather than a victor over the day. I am challenged by these timely words from the Book of Hebrews:

> But encourage one another day after day, as long as it is still called '*Today*,' lest any one of you be hardened by the deceitfulness of sin (Hebrews 3:13).

My prayer is that you and I will not become crusty, miserable and empty old people because of a lifetime of bad choices. We can change that by practicing these simple principles for having a G.R.E.A.T. day for all of the days God gives us. By now, these should be indelibly imprinted on our brains and, hopefully, on the tablets of our hearts:

    G = GREET the day with PRAISE.
    R = REPORT to the day with PURPOSE.
    E = ENGAGE the day with a PLAN.
    A = ANALYZE the day with PERSPECTIVE.
    T = TERMINATE the day with PRAYER.

IT ALL STARTED ONE DAY

I was a premature baby and spent my first six weeks of life in an incubator, with doctors expecting I would not survive. In fact, it was not until I was in my forties, I learned the actual day on which I was born. However, I do know the actual day when I was born-again. It was November 17, 1971—the best day of my life. That is the day I trusted in the Crucified and Risen Lord Jesus Christ as my Savior. You might say that my life story could be titled: *"From an Incubator to the Pulpit—One Day at a Time."*

    I recently read a touching eulogy as a friend spoke of the deceased as a man "on a mission to go from his best interpretation of what the Bible says to his best imitation of how Jesus lived." Oh, how I would want that to be said of you and me.

    Given the way some of our lives are unfolding, we have a lot of work to do for a statement like that to be true. It is a life message that begins with a renewed passion. In the words of C.S. Lewis: "You can't go back and change the beginning, but you can start where you are and change the ending."

I do not know whether I will be around tomorrow, but I do know how to make it through today. I must do so, holding on to the promise given to Ruth by the women of old as she entered a new phase of her life:

> Blessed is the LORD who has not left you without a redeemer *today* and may his name become famous . . . . (Ruth 4:14).

May our blessed Redeemer help us to do TODAY well, knowing He will be with us every moment. May our daily lives make Him famous for generations!

A BLESSED DAY IN THE LIFE OF . . .

The following is a record of one of my recent days. There was nothing particularly noteworthy about it. That's the point. It was a rather typical day. However, I hope this journal shows how easy it can be to follow the principles presented in this book, even to make them a daily habit for a lifetime.

Saturday, October 12th

G. I <u>GREETED</u> THE DAY WITH <u>PRAISE</u>

I woke up at "dark-thirty," maybe around 5 a.m. My first words were, "Thank you, Lord, for this new day. May I serve You well today." I reached into the "country-coffee-cup" drawer and pulled out a cup—this time one from the Philippines. As I made my coffee, I prayed for the many Christians and ministries I know in that land. I also prayed for my family, some by name.

I sat in my easy chair, drinking my coffee and quietly began to get my "praise brain" working with the initial letters of Alphabetical Worship: "Thank You, Lord, that You are ALMIGHTY...BE with me today...etc." (I do not remember how far I got.)

I opened my Bible to my on-going reading, this time in the Book of Jeremiah. As I often do, I prayed God would speak to my heart. He did. I was blessed by the familiar, life-focusing words in Jeremiah 9:23-24:

> Thus says the LORD, "Let not a wise man boast of his wisdom, and let not the mighty man boast of his might, let not a rich man boast of his riches; but let him who boasts boast of this, that he understands and knows Me, that I am the LORD who exercises lovingkindness, justice and righteousness on earth; for I delight in these things," declares the LORD (Jeremiah 9:23-24).

R. I <u>REPORTED</u> TO THE DAY WITH <u>PURPOSE</u>

With those verses in Jeremiah floating through my mind, I got dressed and ate a small breakfast. I was tempted to move on to "the list" but I was drawn to practice what I preach. I stopped to briefly remind myself of who I am and what God called me to be and do *today*. The words "I am a Beloved Child of God, a Soldier of the Cross, a Servant of God, an Ambassador of Jesus Christ, and a Messenger of the Gospel" did not actually come to mind but they were certainly in my thoughts as I sought to face another day in the hope of fulfilling "the purpose of God" in my generation (cf. Acts 13:36).

I was also well aware that "I am a Husband"—married to my girlfriend of almost fifty years. Without saying a word, she gently hovered over me as I finished eating. I laughed as I spoke to her, "Apparently you have some things for me to do for you today." She smiled. That was enough. I was now ready to engage the day.

E. I <u>ENGAGED</u> THE DAY WITH A <u>PLAN</u>

The day before I had sorted out my list of things to do, in specific categories. I now added my wife's Honey Do List and subtracted some things that needed to be moved to my "Future Things to Do" list. Today's itinerary included doing chores, running errands, studying, writing, making numerous ministry calls, as well as following up on some church administration.

It was, as usual, a day of accomplishments, disappointments, distractions and divine appointments. We even had a glorious interruption when a couple of grandkids came by our home for a hug, some laughs and, of course, a few of Grammy's treats. Later that evening I got to do a "would like to do" and ate some of my favorite black licorice—too much, I admit.

A. I <u>ANALYZED</u> THE DAY WITH <u>PERSPECTIVE</u>

Honestly, I didn't evaluate my day as thoroughly as I should have. I did, however, "remark about the remarkable" as I praised God for the surprise visit by my loving grandchildren and my sweet daughter. I also felt good about what I accomplished today. Did everything get done as I wanted? Were my attitudes and actions always the best? Of course not. Such is my life. I will strive to do better tomorrow if, Lord-willing, He gives me another day.

T. I **TERMINATED** THE DAY WITH **PRAYER**

After an early dinner, I read some news and a few emails, watched a science fiction television show, briefly played a computer fishing game (the easiest kind of fishing there is!) and went to sleep around 9:00 p.m. As I put my head on the pillow, I said goodnight to my wife and whispered the evening prayer of Nehemiah 1:11: "...make Your servant successful *today"*—of course, meaning *tomorrow*.

At 12:55 a.m. I woke up without an alarm. I thought of the words of Psalm 119:164 and 119:62: "Seven times a day I praise You" and "At midnight I shall rise to give thanks to You." After a minute or two of praise, I decided to get up. I sat in my easy chair for a *Selah Moment* of quiet, reflecting on the day I had just finished. In other words, I was doing what I should have done the evening before. I made some notes and went back to bed thirty minutes later. I spent the next sleepless hour reading more news and praying through the troubling current events. Oh, how I needed that!

At 5:30 a.m. the alarm went off and I began the day with, admittedly, a somewhat groggy time of prayer and praise: "Lord, I am really tired...but...this is the day You have made; I will choose to rejoice and be glad in it." I reviewed my sermon notes as I prepared my heart and mind to preach at two morning worship services and lead an evening gathering on the church lawn.

Nothing earth-shattering or movie-script worthy happened on October 12th. It was just another day in the divinely-ordained number of days I have left. However, it was truly a G.R.E.A.T. day in my journey to have a full life living *unum diem ad tempus*—one day at a time. For that opportunity, I am eternally grateful.

TODAY'S ASSIGNMENT

1. Do a one-day journal, using the G.R.E.A.T. Day outline.

2. Reflect on the following <u>declaration</u> made by the people of God:

"<u>You have today declared the LORD to be your God</u>, and that you would walk in His ways and keep His statutes, His commandments and His ordinances, and listen to His voice" (Deuteronomy 26:17).

3. Reflect on God's <u>response</u> to their declaration:

"<u>The LORD has today declared you to be His people</u>, a treasured possession, as He promised you, and that you should keep all His commandments; and that He will set you high above all nations which He has made, for praise, fame, and honor; and that you shall be a consecrated people to the LORD your God, as He has spoken" (Deuteronomy 26:18-19).

TOMORROW'S OPPORTUNITIES

1. Do a seven-day journal, using the G.R.E.A.T. Day outline.

2. Review all of the verses in this book, underlining the ones that most speak to your heart.

3. Take a quick glance at all of the studies and worksheets in the appendices. Decide which ones would be of interest for further study. List the appendices and page numbers below:

APPENDIX ONE

PERSONAL AND GROUP STUDY GUIDE

Do the "Today's Assignment" at the end of each section and chapter using the following schedule. Decide whether you will also do the suggested items for further study in "Tomorrow's Opportunities."

Week 1: Introduction: I Want to "Today" Well

Week 2: Chapter Two: Greet the Day with Praise

Week 3: Chapter Three: Report to the Day with Purpose

Week 4: Chapter Four: Engage the Day with a Plan

Week 5: Chapter Five: Analyze the Day with Perspective

Week 6: Chapter Six: Terminate the Day with Prayer

Week 7: Conclusion (The Beginning): Seize the Day

Week 8: Appendices

Read and discuss the value of <u>each</u> of the worksheets and studies. Pick one or two to work on this week individually or as a group.

APPENDIX TWO

PREPARING MY HEART TO WORSHIP DAILY

(AN OVERVIEW OF PSALM 95)

O come, let us sing for joy to the LORD,
Let us shout joyfully to the rock of our salvation.
Let us come before His presence with thanksgiving,
Let us shout joyfully to Him with psalms.
For the LORD is a great God
And a great King above all gods,
In whose hand are the depths of the earth,
The peaks of the mountains are His also.
The sea is His, for it was He who made it,
And His hands formed the dry land.
Come, let us worship and bow down,
Let us kneel before the LORD our Maker.
For He is our God,
And we are the people of His pasture and the sheep of His hand.
Today, if you would hear His voice,
Do not harden your hearts, as at Meribah,
As in the day of Meribah in the wilderness,
When your fathers tested Me,
They tried Me, though they had seen My work.
For forty years I loathed that generation,
And said they are a people who err in their heart,
And they do not know My ways.
Therefore I swore in My anger,
Truly they shall not enter into My rest.
   (Psalm 95, New American Standard Version)

I. The Call to Worship

Psalm 95:1-2 "O come, let us sing for joy to the LORD. Let us shout joyfully to the rock of our salvation. Let us come before His presence with thanksgiving. Let us shout joyfully to Him with psalms."

> **Practice #1. "O come, let us sing for joy to the LORD" (Psalm 95:1).**

Hebrew = *ranan* = *to creak*/sing aloud with shrill sounds (Yes, even bad singing can be sweet music to God's ears)

> **Practice #2. "Let us shout joyfully to the rock of our salvation" (Psalm 95:1).**

shout = Hebrew: *ruwah* = to split the ears with a shrill sound ("make a joyful noise" King James Version)

Psalm 47:1 "Clap your hands, all people; shout to God with the voice of joy." ("a voice of triumph" King James Version).

> **Practice #3. "Let us come before His presence with thanksgiving" (Psalm 95:2).**

Psalm 95:2 "Let US come before His presence with thanksgiving."

> **Practice #4. "Let us shout joyfully to Him <u>with psalms</u>" (Psalm 95:2).**

Psalm 118:24 "This is the day which the LORD has made; let us rejoice and be glad in it." ("Let us stand up and cheer the day the Lord has made.")

I Thessalonians 5:18 ". . .in everything give thanks; for this is God's will for you in Christ Jesus."

Hebrews 13:15 "Through Him then, let us continually offer up a sacrifice of praise to God, that is, the fruit of lips that give thanks to His name."

II. The Motivation for Worship

Motivation #1. A Constant Awareness of the Greatness of God

Psalm 95:3 "For the LORD is a great God and a great King above all gods..."

What is it that clouds that awareness of the glory of God? Idolatry! An idol is anything in our lives that has more of our attention than God.

Some of Our Idols (cf. Colossians 3:5-11)
• Immorality • Impurity • Passion • Evil Desire • Greed
• Anger • Wrath • Malice • Slander • Abusive Speech • Lying

Motivation #2. A Constant Awareness of the Power of the Creator

Psalm 95:4-5 "In whose hand are the depths of the earth, the peaks of the mountains are His also. The sea is His, for it was He who made it, and His hands formed the dry land."

Divine Observation Points

Observation Point #1. Look down at "the depths of the earth" (Psalm 95:4).

Observation Point #2. Look up at "the peaks of the mountains" (Psalm 95:4).

Psalm 121:1-2 "I will lift up my eyes to the mountains; from where shall my help come? My help comes from the LORD, who made heaven and earth."

Observation Point #3. Look deeply at the wonders of "the sea" (Psalm 95:5).

Psalm 95:5 "The sea is His, for it was He who made it."

Observation Point #4. Look around at the beauty of the earth (i.e. "the dry land") **(Psalm 95:5).**

III. The Practice of Worship

#1. Respond to Him as <u>Our Maker</u>

Psalm 95:6 "Come, let us worship and bow down, let us kneel before the LORD our Maker."

"And what do you do when you are confronted with a God too big? You get as low as you can before a God too awesome to grasp. And in that smallness, you say, "Wow!" Then again you may not say anything. Worship is not so much words as it is an automatic response out of your own utter smallness to a God too big—too big to wrap your mind around, too big to figure out . . . . If you found yourself before a giant, would you stand tall, trying to stretch high in order to feel more comfortable, or would you find yourself hunching your shoulders, feeling pressed down even lower by such immensity? Before a God too big the only place to be is as low as you can get." ("What Do You Do with A God Too Big?" by David Needham, Moody Monthly, January 1984)

#2. Acknowledge Him as <u>Our Shepherd</u>

Psalm 95:7 "For He is our God, and we are the people of His pasture and the sheep of His hand."

#3. Obey Him as <u>Our Lord</u>

Psalm 95:7 ". . .Today, if you would hear His voice. . ."

How Do We Listen to God's Voice?

- Spend time <u>today</u> in His Word.

- Be led <u>today</u> by His Holy Spirit.

- Listen <u>today</u> to the godly counsel of others, especially those who are hearing His voice and being led by His Holy Spirit.

IV. The Threat to Worship

Psalm 95:8-11 Do not harden your hearts, as at Meribah, as in the day of Massah in the wilderness, when your fathers tested Me. They tried Me, though they had seen My work. For forty years I loathed that generation, and said they are a people who err in their heart, and they do not know My ways. Therefore I swore in My anger. Truly they shall not enter into My rest.

Exodus 17:7 "He [Moses] named the place Massah (meaning "testing") and Meribah (meaning "rebellion") because of the quarrel of the sons of Israel, and because they tested the LORD, saying, "Is the LORD among us, or not?"

Where are your Massah and Meribah experiences? When were those times when you disobeyed God? When were your seasons of rebellion? (cf. 1 Corinthians 10:6-14).

A Timeline of God's Faithfulness

Complete the following, giving testimony of how God has taken care of you.

• Before I was born, God…

• At the time of my birth, God…

• In the years following, God…

• Today, God…

Psalm 118:1 "Give thanks to the LORD, for He is good; for His lovingkindness is everlasting."

Regarding Entering His Rest (cf. Hebrews 3-4)

© Dr. James M. Cecy, Fresno, CA.

APPENDIX THREE

DEVELOPING A HEART FOR MORNING DEVOTION

(AN OVERVIEW OF PSALM 5:1-3)

Give ear to my words, O LORD,
Consider my groaning.
Heed the sound of my cry for help, my King and my God,
For to You I pray.
In the morning, O LORD, You will hear my voice;
In the morning I will order my prayer to You and eagerly watch.
      (Psalm 5:1-3, New American Standard Version)

>   Psalm 30:5 "...a shout of joy comes <u>in the morning.</u>"
>
>   Psalm 59:16 "...I shall joyfully sing of Your lovingkindness <u>in the morning</u>..."
>
>   Psalm 88:13 ". . .<u>in the morning</u> my prayer comes before You."
>
>   Psalm 90:14 "O satisfy us <u>in the morning</u> with Your lovingkindness, that we may sing for joy and be glad all our days."
>
>   Psalm 92:2 ". . .declare Your lovingkindness <u>in the morning</u>. . ."
>
>   Psalm 143:8 "Let me hear Your lovingkindness <u>in the morning</u>. . ."

Morning Devotion Principle #1. Wake up aware that God wants to hear from you.

>   Psalm 5:1a "Give ear to my words, O LORD. . ."

Psalm 54:2 "Hear my prayer, O God; Give ear <u>to the words of my mouth</u>."

Morning Devotion Principle #2. Share with God your deepest feelings every morning.

Psalm 5:1b "Consider my groaning."
(cf. Romans 8:26-27)

Morning Devotion Principle #3. Be honest about what you really need.

Psalm 5:2a "Heed the sound of my cry for help, my King and my God. . ."

Psalm 88:13 ". . .I cry to you for help, LORD; in the morning my prayer comes before you." (cf. Psalm 46)

Psalm 55:17 "Evening and morning and at noon, I will complain and murmur, and He will hear my voice."

Jeremiah 29:11 "For I know the plans that I have for you, declares the LORD, plans for welfare and not for evil, to give you a future and a hope."

Morning Devotion Principle #4. Keep reminding yourself to whom you are praying.

Psalm 5:2a "Heed the sound of my cry for help, <u>my King and my God. For to You I pray</u>."

Psalm 121:1-3 "I will lift up my eyes to the mountains; From where shall my help come? My help comes from the LORD, who made heaven and earth. He will not allow your foot to slip; He who keeps you will not slumber.

Morning Devotion Principle #5. Pray in the morning when you need it most.

Psalm 5:3a "In the morning, O LORD, You will hear my voice. . ."

> Psalm 119:147 "I rise before dawn and cry for help; I have put my hope in your word."
>
> Mark 1:35 "In the early morning, while it was still dark, Jesus got up, left the house, and went away to a secluded place, and was praying there."

"An hour in the morning is worth two in the evening. While the dew is on the grass, let grace drop upon the soul. Let us give to God the mornings of our days and the mornings of our lives. Prayer should be the key of the day and the lock of the night. Devotion should be both the morning star and the evening star." (C.H. Spurgeon)

Morning Devotion Principle #6. Organize your morning prayer-time.

> Psalm 5:3b ". . .In the morning I will order my prayer to You. . ."

Suggestions for "ordering" prayers. . . (e.g. prayer lists, journals, hymnals, Bible reading plans, praying through Scripture, formal prayers, creeds, etc.)

(For further study refer to Appendix Seven: "Principles for Effective P.R.A.Y.E.R." and Appendix Eight: "Roadblocks to an Effective Prayer-Life.")

Morning Devotion Principle #7. Wait expectantly for God's answers.

> Psalm 5:3c ". . .and eagerly watch." (i.e. look out and up.)

1 John 5:14-15 "This is the confidence which we have before Him, that, if we ask anything according to His will, He hears us. And if we know that He hears us in whatever we ask, we know that we have the requests which we have asked from Him."

John 14:13-14 "Whatever you ask in My name (i.e. consistent with His character and will), that will I do, so that the Father may be glorified in the Son. If you ask Me anything in My name, I will do it."

"How can we expect the Lord to open the windows of his grace, and pour us out a blessing, if we will not open the windows of expectation and look up for the promised favour?" (C.H. Spurgeon)

Psalm 5:4-12 "For You are not a God who takes pleasure in wickedness. No evil dwells with You. The boastful shall not stand before Your eyes. You hate all who do iniquity. You destroy those who speak falsehood. The LORD abhors the man of bloodshed and deceit. But as for me, by Your abundant lovingkindness I will enter Your house, at Your holy temple I will bow in reverence for You. O LORD, lead me in Your righteousness because of my foes. Make Your way straight before me. There is nothing reliable in what they say. Their inward part is destruction *itself.* Their throat is an open grave. They flatter with their tongue. Hold them guilty, O God. By their own devices let them fall! In the multitude of their transgressions thrust them out, for they are rebellious against You. But let all who take refuge in You be glad. Let them ever sing for joy, and may You shelter them that those who love Your name may exult in You. For it is You who blesses the righteous man, O LORD. You surround him with favor as with a shield."

Joshua 24:15 "As for me and my house, we will serve the LORD."

Lamentations 3:22-23 "The steadfast love of the LORD never ceases; his mercies never come to an end; they are new every morning; great is your faithfulness." (English Standard Version)

> *Give ear to my words, O LORD,*
> *Consider my meditation.*
> *Hearken unto the voice of my cry,*
> *My King, and my God:*
> *For unto Thee will I pray.*
> *My voice shalt Thou hear in the morning,*
> *O LORD; in the morning*
> *Will I direct my prayer*
> *Unto Thee, and will look up.*
> *(Psalm 5:1-3, King James Version)*

© Dr. James M. Cecy, Fresno, CA

APPENDIX FOUR

ALPHABETICAL WORSHIP WORKSHEET

Use the alphabetical list below to state some of your praises for today. Use this throughout the day:

"Thank You, Lord for…" "I praise You for being…"
"Today, I praise you for…" "Today, I am grateful for…"

A. N.

B. O.

C. P.

D. Q.

E. R.

F. S.

G. T.

H. U.

I. V.

J. W.

K. X.

L. Y.

M. Z

My Other Expressions of Praise and Thanksgiving for Today:

APPENDIX FIVE

WORKSHEET FOR RESOLVING A CONFLICT

Briefly describe the specific nature of the conflict:

Instructions for Using this Worksheet

1. Read thoughtfully through the list of "one another verses."
2. Place an X next to those you feel the other person has violated in your conflict.
3. Put an O next to those you feel you have violated in your conflict with the other person.
4. In the space between each of the points write some specific and personal application to your present conflict with the other person.
5. Use these as discussion points.

Confess your faults to one another (James 5:16).

Be of the same mind toward one another (Romans 12:16).

Forgive one another (Colossians 3:13; Ephesians 4:32).

Submit to one another (Ephesians 5:21; 1 Peter 5:5).

Restore one another (Galatians 6:1).

Bear one another's burdens (Galatians 6:2).

Receive (welcome) one another (Romans 15:7).

Greet one another (Romans 16:16; 1 Peter 5:14; 1 Corinthians 16:20).

Edify (build up) one another (Romans 14:9).

Love (self-sacrifice for) one another (Romans 12:9-10; 1 Peter 4:8; John 13:34; 15:12-17).

Teach and exhort one another (Colossians 3:13, 16; Hebrews 3:13).

Admonish (warn) one another (Romans 15:14).

Rebuke one another (Luke 17:3).

Contribute to the (financial) needs of one another (Romans 12:13).

Encourage one another (1 Thessalonians 5:11; Hebrews 10:25).

Pray for one another (James 5:16).

Comfort one another (1 Thessalonians 4:18).

Stimulate one another to love and good deeds (Hebrews 10:24).

Use your gifts to serve one another (1 Peter 4:10; Galatians 5:13).

Be at peace with one another (Mark 9:50).

WORKSHEET FOR RESOLVING A CONFLICT

Wash one another's feet (i.e. be a Christ-like servant toward the other) (John 13:14).

Be hospitable to one another (1 Peter 4:9; Romans 12:13).

Be kind to one another (Ephesians. 4:32).

Give preference to one another (Romans 12:10).

Regard one another as more important than yourself (Philippians 2:3).

Be tenderhearted toward one another (Ephesians 4:32).

Don't bite and devour one another (Galatians 5:15).

Don't cause one another to stumble (to sin) (Romans 14:13; 1 Corinthians 12:25).

Don't provoke one another (Galatians 5:26).

Don't lie to one another (Colossians 3:9).

Don't envy one another (Galatians 5:26).

Don't hate one another (Titus 3:3).

Don't speak evil against one another (James 4:11).

Don't complain against one another (James 5:9).

Don't judge one another (Matthew 7:1; Romans 14:13).

Now go to that person TODAY and do what you know God wants you to do!

Ephesians 4:26-27 "In your anger do not sin; do not let the sun go down while you are still angry, and do not give the devil a foothold." (New International Version)

James 1:19-22 "My dear brothers, take note of this: Everyone should be quick to listen, slow to speak and slow to become angry, for man's anger does not bring about the righteous life that God desires . . . Do not merely listen to the word, and so deceive yourselves. Do what it says." (New International Version)

James 4:1-3 "What causes fights and quarrels among you? Don't they come from your desires that battle within you? You want something but don't get it. You kill and covet, but you cannot have what you want. You quarrel and fight. You do not have, because you do not ask God." (New International Version)

© Dr. James M. Cecy, Fresno, CA.

APPENDIX SIX

GOD HAS SPOKEN IN HIS MARVELOUS WORD

(An Overview of Psalm 19:7-14)

- God is calling us to stand, without compromise, on the truths of the Word of God as our only true source of faith and practice.

Deuteronomy 29:29 "The secret things belong to the LORD our God, but the things revealed belong to us and to our sons forever, that we may observe all the words of this law."

- We exist to bring glory to God and have our lives changed by the Word of God.

> Psalm 19:1-6 "God has Spoken in His Mighty Works."
> Psalm 19:7-14 "God has Spoken in His Marvelous Word."

Psalm 19:7-14

The law of the LORD is perfect, restoring the soul. The testimony of the Lord is sure, making wise the simple. The precepts of the LORD are right, rejoicing the heart. The commandment of the LORD is pure, enlightening the eyes. The fear of the LORD is clean, enduring forever. The judgments of the LORD are true; they are righteous altogether. They are more desirable than gold, yes, than much fine gold; sweeter also than honey and the drippings of the honeycomb. Moreover, by them Your servant is warned. In keeping them there is great reward. Who can discern his errors? Acquit me of hidden faults. Also keep back Your servant from presumptuous sins. Let them not rule over me. Then I will be blameless, and I shall be acquitted of great transgression. Let the words of my mouth and the meditation of my heart be acceptable in Your sight, O LORD, my rock and my Redeemer.

I. David's Detailed Description of the Word of God (Psalm 19:7-9)

Psalm 19:7-9 "The law of the LORD is perfect, restoring the soul; The testimony of the LORD is sure, making wise the simple. The precepts of the LORD are right, rejoicing the heart; The commandment of the Lord is pure, enlightening the eyes. The fear of the Lord is clean, enduring forever. The judgments of the Lord are true; they are righteous altogether."

A. Six Facets of the Word of God

Facet #1. The Word of God presents us with the LAW of the Lord.

Facet #2. The Word of God presents us with the TESTIMONY of the Lord.

Facet #3. The Word of God presents us with the PRECEPTS of the Lord.

Facet #4. The Word of God presents us with the COMMANDS of the Lord.

Facet #5. The Word of God presents us with the FEAR of the Lord.

Facet #6. The Word of God presents us with the JUDGMENTS of the Lord.

B. Six Characteristics of the Word of God

1. The Word of God is PERFECT.
2. The Word of God is SURE.
3. The Word of God is RIGHT.
4. The Word of God is PURE.
5. The Word of God is CLEAN.
6. The Word of God is TRUE.

2 Timothy 3:16-17 "All Scripture is inspired by God (i.e. God-breathed) and profitable for teaching, for reproof, for correction, for training in righteousness; so that the man of God may be adequate, equipped for every good work."

Hebrews 4:12 "For the word of God is living and active and sharper than any two-edged sword, and piercing as far as the division of soul and spirit, of both joints and marrow, and able to judge the thoughts and intentions of the heart."

C. Six Ways the Word of God Impacts Our Lives

1. The Word of God RESTORES THE SOUL.
2. The Word of God MAKES WISE THE SIMPLE.
3. The Word of God REJOICES THE HEART.
4. The Word of God ENLIGHTENS THE EYES.
5. The Word of God ENDURES FOREVER.
6. The Word of God IS ALTOGETHER RIGHTEOUS.

II. David's Deep-Seated Attraction to the Word of God (Psalm 19:10-11)

Testimony #1 "The Word of God is more desirable to me than riches."

Psalm 19:10 "They are more desirable than gold, yes, than much fine gold..."

Psalm 119:14 "I have rejoiced in the way of Your testimonies, as much as in all riches."

Psalm 119:72 "The law of Your mouth is better to me than thousands of gold and silver pieces."

Psalm 119:127 "Therefore I love Your commandments above gold, yes, above fine gold."

Testimony #2. "The Bible is sweeter than the sweetest thing in my life."

Psalm 19:10 "...sweeter also than honey and the drippings of the honeycomb."

Psalm 119:103 "How sweet are Your words to my taste! Yes, sweeter than honey to my mouth!"

Testimony #3. "The Word of God is the source of valuable protection in my life."

Psalm 19:11 "Moreover, by them Your servant is warned..."

Psalm 119:9-11 "How can a young man keep his way pure? By keeping it according to Your word. With all my heart I have sought You; do not let me wander from Your commandments. Your word I have treasured in my heart, <u>that I may not sin against You</u>."

Testimony #4. "The Word of God is the source of great reward in my life."

Psalm 19:11 "...in keeping them there is great reward."

Joshua 1:8 "This book of the law shall not depart from your mouth, but you shall meditate on it day and night, so that you may be careful to do according to all that is written in it; for then you will make your way prosperous, <u>and then you will have success</u>."

Psalm 1:2-3 "But his delight is in the law of the LORD, and in His law he meditates day and night. He will be like a tree firmly planted by streams of water, which yields its fruit in its season and its leaf does not wither; and <u>in whatever he does, he prospers</u>."

III. David's Desperate Conviction Regarding the Word of God (Psalm 19:12-13)

Psalm 19:12-13 "Who can discern his errors? Acquit me of hidden faults. Also keep back Your servant from presumptuous sins; let them not rule over me; then I will be blameless, and I shall be acquitted of great transgression."

Hebrews 4:13 "And there is no creature hidden from His sight, but all things are open and laid bare to the eyes of Him with whom we have to do."

Psalm 51:1-2 "Be gracious to me, O God, according to Your lovingkindness; according to the greatness of Your compassion blot out my transgressions. Wash me thoroughly from my iniquity and cleanse me from my sin."

Psalm 139:23-24 "Search me, O God, and know my heart; try me and know my anxious thoughts; and see if there be any hurtful way in me, and lead me in the everlasting way."

"The Bible will keep you from sin or sin will keep you from the Bible." (D.L. Moody)

IV. David's Daily Devotion to the God of the Bible (Psalm 19:14)

Psalm 19:14 "Let the words of my mouth and the meditation of my heart be acceptable in Your sight, O LORD, my rock and my Redeemer."

The Challenge:

The road to becoming a man or woman of the Word begins with a journey of the heart!

1 Corinthians 1:14-16 "But a natural man does not accept the things of the Spirit of God, for they are foolishness to him; and he cannot understand them, because they are spiritually appraised. But he who is spiritual appraises all things, yet he himself is appraised by no one. For who has known the mind of the Lord, that He will instruct Him? But we have the mind of Christ."

Ecclesiastes 12:11-14 "The words of wise men are like goads, and masters of these collections are like well-driven nails; they are given by one Shepherd. But beyond this, my son, be warned: the writing of many books is endless, and excessive devotion to books is wearying to the body. The conclusion, when all has been heard, is: fear God and keep His commandments, because this applies to every person. For God will bring every act to judgment, everything which is hidden, whether it is good or evil."

2 Timothy 2:15 "Be diligent to present yourself approved to God as a workman who does not need to be ashamed, handling accurately the word of truth."

© Dr. James M. Cecy, Fresno, CA.

APPENDIX SEVEN

PRINCIPLES FOR EFFECTIVE P.R.A.Y.E.R.

(Adapted from Jesus' instruction on prayer in Matthew 6:9-13, King James Version)

P = PRAISING God in words and song for who He is and what He has done

> *"Our Father which art in heaven, hallowed be thy name, thy kingdom come..." (Matthew 6:9-10, KJV)*

R = REPENTING of those things that offend God

> *"...forgive us our debts, as we forgive our debtors..." (Matthew 6:12, KJV)*

A = ASKING specifically for the things I need

> *"Give us this day our daily bread." (Matthew 6:11, KJV)*

Y = YIELDING to His will in every area of my life

> *"Thy will be done in earth as it is in heaven..." (Matthew 6:10, KJV)*

E = ENTREATING for others

> *"Give US...forgive US...lead US not...deliver US..." (Matthew 6:11, 12, 13, KJV)*

R = REJOICING, in advance, for what God is going to do

> *"For thine is the kingdom, and the power, and the glory, for ever. Amen." (Matthew 6:13, KJV)*

© Dr. James M. Cecy, Fresno, CA.

APPENDIX EIGHT

ROADBLOCKS TO AN EFFECTIVE PRAYER-LIFE

Introduction:

Hebrews 12:1-2 "...let us lay aside every encumbrance, and the sin which so easily entangles us, and let us run with endurance the race that is set before us, fixing our eyes on Jesus, the author and perfecter of faith..."

"encumbrance" = Greek: *ogkos* (pronounced onkos) = a heavy weight, a major hindrance, a roadblock

Luke 11:1 "Lord, teach us to pray."

P.R.A.Y.E.R. = Praising • Repenting • Asking • Yielding • Entreating • Rejoicing

(For further study see Appendix Seven: "Principles for Effective P.R.A.Y.E.R.")

Colossians 4:2 "Devote yourselves to prayer, keeping alert in it with an attitude of thanksgiving."

Roadblock #1. Unbelief hinders prayer

    A. The Principle: I must be a born-again child of God in order to be effective in prayer.

Apart from the prayers that come from a truth-seeking heart, open to salvation in Jesus Christ (Jeremiah 29; Matthew 7, etc.), God does not necessarily hear the general prayers of an unbeliever.

    B. The Biblical Proof

Job 27:8-10: "For what is the hope of the godless...will God hear his cry?" (The implied answer is: "No!") "...will he (i.e. the unbeliever) call on God at all times?" (The implied answer: "Most likely but God will not answer the call!")

Proverbs 15:8b "The sacrifice (i.e. the meaningless worship) of the wicked is an abomination to the LORD but the prayer of the upright is His delight."

Proverbs 15:29 "The LORD is far from the wicked. But He hears the prayer of the righteous."

Psalm 145:18-19 "The LORD is near to those who call on Him in truth."

Matthew, Chapter 6 refers to God as our Father some numerous times. Yet no one can come to the Father except through Jesus Christ who is the way, the truth and the life (John 14:6).

Roadblock #2. Sin hinders prayer

    A. The Principle: I must be dealing with sin in order to be effective in prayer.

    B. The Biblical Proof

Lamentations 3:8-9 "Even when I cry out and call for help, He shuts out my prayer. He has blocked my ways…"

James 5:16b "The effective prayer of a righteous man can accomplish much."

    (1) The SIN of disobedience hinders my prayer-life.

Proverbs 28:9 "He who turns away his ear from listening to the law, even his prayer is an abomination."

Psalm 66:18 "If I regard wickedness in my heart, the LORD will not hear."

Psalm 109:7 "And let his prayer become sin."

(2) The SIN of idolatry hinders my prayer-life.

Colossians 3:5-8 "Therefore consider the members of your earthly body as dead to immorality, impurity, passion, evil desire and greed, which amounts to idolatry. For it is on account of these things that the wrath of God will come upon the sons of disobedience, and in them you also once walked, when you were living in them. But now you also, put them all aside: anger, wrath, malice, slander, and abusive speech from your mouth."

(3) The SIN of pride hinders my prayer-life.

Job 35:12-13 "There they cry out, but He does not answer because of the pride of evil men. Surely God will not listen to an empty cry. Nor will the Almighty regard it."

2 Chronicles 7:14 "...if my people who are called by My name will humble themselves and pray and turn from their wicked ways, then I will hear from heaven, will forgive their sin and will heal their land."

Roadblock #3. Hypocrisy hinders prayer

    A. The Principle: I must be dealing with the inconsistencies in my life in order to be effective in prayer.

    B. The Biblical Proof

        (1) Not being honest <u>with myself</u> hinders my prayer-life.

Isaiah 1:10ff. speaks of how much God hated all the offerings, sacrifices and religious observances of hypocritical Israel.

        (2) Not being honest <u>with others</u> hinders my prayer-life.

             (a) The dishonesty of praying to be seen by men.

Matthew 6:5 "And when you pray, you are not to be as the hypocrites, for they love to stand and pray in the synagogues and on the street corners, in order to be seen by men. Truly I say to you, they have their reward in full."

> **(b) The phoniness of refusing to admit and confess our faults to one another.**

James 5:16a "Therefore, confess your sins to one another, and pray for one another, so that you may be healed."

> **(3) Not being honest <u>with God</u> hinders my prayer-life.**

cf. Psalm 10:1; 22:1; 22:2; 42:6 and the honesty of Hannah, Moses, David, and Job, etc.

Roadblock #4. Asking with wrong motives hinders prayer

> **A. The Principle: I must evaluate my motives in order to be effective in prayer.**
>
> **B. The Biblical Proof**
>
> > **(1) Pleasure-seeking hinders my prayer-life.**

James 4:3 "You ask and do not receive, because you ask with wrong motives, so that you may spend it on your pleasures."

> > **(2) Not wanting God's will hinders my prayer-life.**

1 John 5:14-15 "And this is the confidence which we have before Him, that if we ask anything <u>according to His will</u>, He hears us. And if we know that He hears us in whatever we ask, we know that we have the requests which we have asked of Him."

> cf. John 14:7ff. where Jesus said, "If you ask anything in My name . . ." (i.e. anything consistent with My will).
>
> > **(3) The love of money hinders my prayer-life.**

cf. Matthew 21:12-17; Luke 19:45-47 regarding a House of Prayer vs. a Den of Thieves

1 Timothy 6:10-11 "For the love of money is a root of all sorts of evil....But flee from these things, you man of God; and pursue righteousness, godliness, faith, love, perseverance and gentleness."

(4) Selective praying hinders my prayer-life.

1 Timothy 2:1 "...I urge that entreaties and prayers, petitions and thanksgivings, be made on behalf of all men..."

1 Samuel 12:23 "Moreover, as for me, far be it from me that I should sin against the LORD by ceasing to pray for you..."

Matthew 5:44-45 "But I say to you, love your enemies, and pray for those who persecute you in order that you may be sons of your Father who is in heaven..."

Roadblock #5. Mistreating people hinders prayer

A. The Principle: I must not think I can hurt people and still be effective in prayer.

B. The Biblical Proof

(1) Mistreating the needy hinders my prayer-life.

Isaiah 1:15-17 "So when you spread out your hands in prayer, I will hide My eyes from you. yes, even though you multiply prayers, I will not listen. Your hands are full of bloodshed. Wash yourselves, make yourselves clean; remove the evil of your deeds from My sight. Cease to do evil, learn to do good; seek justice; reprove the ruthless; defend the orphan, plead for the widow."

James 1:27 "This is pure and undefiled religion in the sight of our God and Father, to visit orphans and widows in their distress, and to keep oneself unstained by the world."

(2) Mistreating workers hinders my prayer-life.

James 5:4 "Behold the pay of the laborers who mowed your fields, and which has been withheld by you, cries out against you; and the outcry of those who did the harvesting has reached the ears of the Lord of Sabaoth."

This matter of mistreating workers also applies to paying what we owe (cf. Romans 13:8).

(3) Mistreating the flock of God hinders my prayer-life.

Ezekiel 34 speaks of the spiritual shepherds who were abusing the flock by not taking proper care of them (cf. 1 Peter 5:1ff.).

Roadblock #6. Mistreating my spouse hinders prayer

A. The Principle: I must honor my spouse in order to be effective in prayer.

B. The Biblical Proof

Malachi 2:13ff. "And this is another thing you do: you cover the altar of the LORD with tears, with weeping and with groaning, because He no longer regards the offering or accepts it with favor from your hand. Yet you say, 'For what reason?' Because the LORD has been a witness between you and the wife of your youth, against whom you have dealt treacherously, though she is your companion and your wife by covenant. . ."

1 Peter 3:7 "You husbands, likewise, live with your wives in an understanding way, as with a weaker vessel, since she is a woman; and grant her honor as a fellow-heir of the grace of life, <u>so that your prayers may not be hindered</u>."

Roadblock #7. Anger and bitterness hinder prayer

A. The Principle: I must deal with my anger and bitterness in order to be effective in prayer.

B. The Biblical Proof

(1) Anger hinders my prayer-life.

1 Timothy 2:8 "...I want men in every place to pray, lifting up holy hands, without wrath and dissention." cf. Colossians 3:5; Ephesians 4:26.

(2) Lack of forgiveness hinders my prayer-life.

Mark 11:25 "And whenever you stand praying, forgive, if you have anything against anyone; so that your Father also who is in heaven may forgive you your transgressions."

Matthew 6:12 "And forgive us our debts, as we also have forgiven our debtors."

Ephesians 4:32 "Be kind to one another, tender-hearted, forgiving each other, just as God in Christ also has forgiven you."

(3) Lack of thanksgiving hinders my prayer-life.

Philippians 4:6 "Be anxious for nothing, but in everything by prayer and supplication with thanksgiving let your requests be made known to God."

Colossians 4:2 "Devote yourselves to prayer, keeping alert in it with an attitude of thanksgiving..."

Roadblock #8. Laziness hinders prayer

A. The Principle: I must be diligent in order to be effective in prayer.

B. The Biblical Proof

(1) Lack of devotion hinders my prayer-life.

Colossians 4:2 speaks of being devoted to (Greek: *proskartereo* = "strongly continue in") the practice of prayer.

2 Timothy 1:3 "...as I constantly remember you in my prayers night and day..."

(2) Not persevering hinders my prayer-life.

Luke 18:1 "Now He [Jesus] was telling them a parable to show that all times they ought to pray <u>and not to lose heart</u>..."

Luke 11:9-10 "And I say to you, ask (lit. keep on asking)...seek (lit. keep on seeking)...knock (lit. keep on knocking), and it shall be opened to you."

1 Thessalonians 5:17 "Pray without ceasing."

cf. Luke 6:12 where Jesus spent the whole night in prayer to God ... rising up even before daybreak to do it (Mark 1:35).

James 5:17-18 speaks of Elijah who "prayed earnestly" and then "prayed again."

In 1 Samuel 1 Hannah cried out to the Lord in what is described as "multiplied prayers."

(3) Vain repetition hinders my prayer-life.

Matthew 6:7 "And when you are praying, do not use meaningless repetition, as the Gentiles do, for they suppose that they will be heard for their many words."

Note: The key here is not repetition but empty, <u>meaningless</u> repetition.

Roadblock #9. Doubt hinders prayer

> **A. The Principle: I must pray with confidence in order to be effective in prayer.**
>
> **B. The Biblical Proof**

James 1:6 "But let him ask in faith, without any doubting, for the one who doubts is like the surf of the sea driven and tossed by the wind. But let not that man expect that he will receive anything from the Lord, being a double-minded man, unstable in all his ways."

Matthew 21:22 "And everything you ask in prayer, believing, you shall receive."

Mark 11:24-25 "Therefore I say to you, whoever says to this mountain, 'Be taken up and cast into the sea,' and does not doubt in his heart, but believes that what he says is going to happen, it shall be granted him. Therefore I say to you, all things for which you pray and ask, believe that you have received them, and they shall be granted you."

Roadblock #10. Lack of physical rest hinders prayer

    A. The Principle: I must be rested if I am going to be effective in prayer.

    B. The Biblical Proof

Colossians 4:2 speaks of <u>keeping alert</u> in prayer.

Luke 22:45-46 "And when He [Jesus] rose from prayer, he came to His disciples and found them sleeping from sorrow, and said to them, "Why are you sleeping? Rise and pray that you may not enter into temptation."

Anytime of the day is a good time to pray.

Mark 1:35 speaks of Jesus rising up to pray "a great while before day."

Psalm 5:3 "<u>In the morning</u>, O LORD, You will hear my voice. <u>In the morning</u> I will order my prayer to You and eagerly watch."

Psalm 141:2 "May my prayer be counted as incense before You; the lifting up of my hands <u>as the evening offering</u>."

Psalm 119:55 "O LORD, I remember Your name <u>in the night</u>."

Psalm 119:62 "<u>At midnight</u> I will rise to give thanks to You."

Psalm 119:164 "Seven times a day I praise You..."

Roadblock #11. Discouragement hinders prayer

    A. The Principle: I must not let my weakness in prayer keep me from being effective in prayer.

B. The Biblical Proof

cf. Luke 18:1ff. where Jesus wanted His disciples to pray and not lose heart.

Jeremiah 29:11-14 "For I know the plans that I have for you," declares the LORD, plans for welfare and not for calamity to give you a future and a hope. Then you will call upon Me and come and pray to Me, and I will listen to you. And you will seek Me and find Me when you search for Me with all your heart. And I will be found by you. . ."

Jeremiah 33:3 "Call to Me, and I will answer you, and I will tell you great and mighty things, which you do not know."

Concluding Challenge:

Isaiah 56:7 "Even those I will bring to my holy mountain, and make them joyful in my house of prayer. . .for My house will be called a house of prayer for all the peoples."

Our Prayer:

"Lord, may our lives, our homes and our churches be Houses of Prayer for all people. Give us the strength to remove the hindrances and restore to us the joy of talking to You as Our Heavenly Father."

© Dr. James M. Cecy, Fresno, CA.

APPENDIX NINE

DAILY BIBLE READING IDEAS

Psalm 119:11 "Your word I have treasured in my heart . . ."

"I have read the Bible through one hundred times,
and always with increasing delight." (George Mueller)

The following ideas for daily Bible reading are only suggestions. Revise them to fit your schedule and style. No matter what method you use, keep a record (perhaps on a blank page in your Bible) and be sure to underline key passages for future reference. Mark any of the following ideas you have used or appeal to you:

- Read the Bible with a loved one.
- Read portions of the Bible you have never or barely read.
- Read through the entire Bible in a year, following any number of yearly reading plans available.
- Read through the entire Bible at your own pace.
- Read through the entire Old Testament.
- Read through the entire New Testament.
- Read through the first books of the Bible (Pentateuch/Torah).
- Read through the twelve historical books (Joshua through Esther).
- Read through the five wisdom books (Psalms through Song of Solomon).
- Read through the five major prophets (Isaiah though Daniel).
- Read through the four gospels (Matthew through John).
- Read through the Book of Acts.
- Read through the epistles of Paul (Romans through Philemon).
- Read through the general epistles (Hebrews through Jude).
- Read through the Book of Revelation.
- Read one book of the Bible every day for one month, going through it as many times as you want.
- Read one of the shorter books (or a short section) of the Bible every day for thirty days.
- Read one chapter of Proverbs every day for one month, underlining your favorite proverb in each chapter.
- Read five Psalms every day for one month, underlining key passages.

- Read your favorite Psalm and the Psalm before and after. (Sometimes they are related.)
- Read Psalm 119 (the longest chapter in the Bible) and underline all references to the value of the Word of God.
- Read Psalm 19:7-14 writing out the key words and phrase related to the value of the Word of God.
- Read Matthew, Chapters 1-2 and Luke, Chapters 1-2 regarding the birth of Christ. Look for things you have never considered before.
- Read the Sermon on the Mount (Matthew 5-7) for a week or a month.
- Read the Beatitudes (Matthew 5:1-12) for a week.
- Read the Parables in the Gospels, especially Matthew and Luke.
- Read the "companion epistles" together, comparing them (e.g. 1 and 2 Corinthians, 1 and 2 Thessalonians, 1 and 2 Timothy, 1 and 2 Peter, 1, 2 and 3 John, Ephesians and Colossians, 2 Peter and Jude, etc.).
- Read Revelation 1-3 (Jesus' letters to the seven churches. (Revelation, Chapter 1 sets the scene for Chapters 2 and 3).
- Read a recommended Study Bible, paying attention to the author's additional notes.
- Study the background and historical information of a Bible book and then read it.
- Read a Bible-based devotional that points you back to Scripture. Look up the verses in your Bible.
- Listen to a message by a trusted Bible teacher and read all the passages mentioned.
- Pick out thirty or thirty-one of your favorite Psalms and read one each day for a month.
- Write out a key verse or passage on which to meditate throughout the day.
- Pray for others using the "prayer-portions" of Scripture (e.g. Ephesians 1:3-14; Colossians 1:9-14, etc.).
- Pray through portions of Scripture, personalizing it for yourself.
- List other suggestions you have used, or you have learned from other trusted sources (e.g. your spiritual mentors).

© Dr. James M. Cecy, Fresno, CA

APPENDIX TEN

A POCKET GUIDE FOR EFFECTIVE BIBLE STUDY

In order to assist you in your personal study, use the following five-step process. (Place this guide before you as you study).

Step One: Preparation - Anticipating God's Direction

1. Begin with P.R.A.Y.E.R. (praising, repenting, asking, yielding, entreating, rejoicing).

2. Make a commitment to strive to find the single meaning of the text.

3. Proceed with caution, drawing conclusions from the facts of Scripture (inductive exegesis).

Step Two: Observation - Asking the Right Questions

1. Study the background of the book. Do a complete survey on the book.

2. Read the entire chapter a number of times in many translations.

3. Examine carefully the specific passage in many translations.

4. Ask appropriate questions (who? what? where? when? how? why?).

5. Look up cross-references.

6. Write down any further observations.

Step Three: Interpretation - Answering the Right Questions

1. Do particular word studies (synonyms, antonyms, figures of speech, idioms, repeated words and phrases, etc.).
2. Watch for specific details in the grammar (tenses, voices, moods, prepositions, conjunctions, etc.).
3. Write down what others say about the text.
4. Begin problem solving, deciding on what seems to be the best view.

Step Four: Application - Applying the Right Answers

1. Answer the question: So what?

2. List commands to obey, promises to keep, truths to know, actions to take, sins to forsake, examples to follow, things to avoid, new thoughts about God.

Step Five: Presentation - Announcing the Good News

1. Keep a notebook and file all research.

2. Share what you have learned with others—soon!

(This Pocket Guide is adapted from *"Mastering the Scriptures: A Self-Study Course in Effective Bible Study"* by Dr. James M. Cecy. Available at www.jaron.org)

© Dr. James M. Cecy, Fresno, CA.

APPENDIX ELEVEN

MY DAILY PRAYER JOURNAL

Date: _____

Things for which I praise God today:

    (See Appendix Four: "Alphabetical Worship Worksheet")

Things I learned about my relationship to God today:

From the Bible (State the text):

From others (State the source):

- Commands to Obey:

- Promises to Keep:

- Truths to Know:

- Actions to Take:

- Sins to Forsake:

- Examples to Follow:

- Things to Avoid:

- New Thoughts about God:

People for Whom I am Praying Today:

• Family:

• Friends:

• Neighbors:

• Church Leaders:

• Missionaries:

• Other Ministries:

• My City:

• My State/Region:

• My Country:

• Other Countries:

Today's Personal Reflections:

APPENDIX TWELVE

MY DAILY PRIORITY LIST

THINGS THAT SHOULD ALWAYS BE ON MY LIST OF THINGS TO DO DAILY

- Spend at least thirty minutes in prayer, praise and reflection from my personal Bible reading.

- Listen to my favorite sacred music. Recite or sing the words of one of my favorite hymns or spiritual songs.

- Tell at least one person "I love you" and "I'm proud of you" and "I appreciate you."

- Exercise for at least 15-30 minutes. (e.g. Walk at least 5,000 to 10,000 steps).

- Eat well. Keep a record.

- Tell one person about Christ.

- Send a word of encouragement to at least three people.

- Greet at least one neighbor and help, where needed.

- Take fifteen minutes for complete silence or take a longer nap.

- Do at least one project I would rather not do.

- Do at least one thing on my "Get Ahead" (Future Project) List.

- Other: _____

Now, here's my list for TODAY:

HAVE A G.R.E.A.T. DAY

MY THINGS TO DO TODAY

Date: _____

Priorities:

The things I <u>must</u> do today ($A_1 A_2 A_3$, etc.)
The things I <u>should</u> do today ($B_1 B_2 B_3$, etc.)
The things I <u>would like</u> to do today ($C_1 C_2 C_3$, etc.)
The things I <u>must do</u> in the future ($D_1 D_2 D_3$, etc.)

Categories:

(e.g. Home, Work, School, Ministry, Calls, Future Projects, etc.)

Category	Priority	Task/Project	Due Date
_____	_____	_____	_____
_____	_____	_____	_____
_____	_____	_____	_____

Notes/Comments:

MY THINGS TO DO TOMORROW AND THE FUTURE

Category	Priority	Task/Project	Due Date
_____	_____	_____	_____
_____	_____	_____	_____
_____	_____	_____	_____

Notes/Comments:

APPENDIX THIRTEEN

HOW DO I MAKE BIBLICAL DECISIONS EVERY DAY?

We know it is God's will that we be filled with the Spirit (Ephesians 5:16-18), thankful (1 Thessalonians 5:18), pure (1 Thessalonians 4:3), submissive to authority (1 Peter 2:13-15), and even willing to suffer (1 Peter 3:17). It is also God's will that we know His will (Ephesians 5:17).

But what about those daily decisions? What do we do? What should we say? Where do we go? How do we choose between things that are good choices? Does God really care about those little decisions, as well?

Ephesians 5:15-17 "Therefore be careful how you walk, not as unwise men, but as wise, making the most of your time because the days are evil. So then do not be foolish, but understand what the will of the Lord is."

I. SEEKING GOD'S WILL THE WRONG WAY

There are three kinds of false-seekers:

1. Those who think God's will is lost and will have difficulty finding it.

"It feels like God is a Cosmic Easter Bunny hiding His perfect will for my life in some remote place."

2. Those who are afraid of God's will.

"It feels like God is a Cosmic Killjoy wanting my life to be miserable because I'm such a sinner."

3. Those who want God's will only if it fits with their desires.

"It feels like God is a Cosmic Genie waiting to grant my every wish."

II. DETERMINING GOD'S WILL IN GENERAL MATTERS OF LIFE

1. It is God's will that we be saved (2 Peter 3:9; John 10:4; Mark 3:31-35).

2. It is God's will that we be filled with the Spirit (Ephesians 5:16-18).

3. It is God's will that we be pure (1 Thessalonians 4:3-7).

4. It is God's will that we be submissive to authority (1 Peter 2:13-15).

5. It is God's will that we be willing to suffer (1 Peter 3:17).

6. It is God's will that we be thankful for our circumstances (1 Thessalonians 5:18).

7. It is God's will that we know His will (Ephesians 5:17).

III. DISCERNING GOD'S WILL IN SPECIFIC SITUATIONS IN LIFE

Once you have considered the above general conditions you may now proceed to the following steps to determine God's will in specific matters. Ask yourself the following questions:

ISSUE #1: WHAT DOES THE BIBLE SAY ABOUT IT?

a. Does it enslave me? Is it profitable for me and others? (1 Corinthians 6:12-13)

b. Will it harm me in any way? (1 Corinthians 6:19-20)

c. Is it characteristic of the world or contrary to God's values? (1 John 2:15-17)

d. Will it cause other believers to stumble? (Romans 14:13-23)

e. Will it cause me to serve the wrong master (i.e. money)? (Matthew 6:24, 33)

f. Would I want to be doing this when Christ returns? (Matthew. 24:44)

g. Is it consistent with Christ's character? Would He do this? (Colossians 3:17)

h. Am I doing this to please men or God? (Colossians 3:23)

ISSUE #2: WHAT DO MY AUTHORITIES AND FRIENDS SAY ABOUT IT?

a. Does God's Word permit it? (2 Timothy 3:16)

b. Does it break any law? (Romans 13:1-7; 1 Peter 2:13-15)

c. Do the elders or spiritual leaders in my local church approve? (1 Peter 5:5; Hebrews 13:17)

d. Do my parents approve? (Ephesians 6:1-3)

e. Does my spouse approve? (Ephesians 5:22; Malachi 2:14-15)

f. Do my close friends approve? (Proverbs 11:14; 15:22; 27:9)

ISSUE #3: AM I WALKING IN THE SPIRIT?

a. Am I experiencing any of the deeds of the flesh? (Galatians 5:19-21)

b. Am I experiencing the fruit of the Spirit? (Galatians 5:22-23)

c. Am I truly yielded to God, desiring to do His will above my own? (Romans 12:1-2)

d. Do I have peace about the decision? (Philippians 4:4-7)

Now comes the exciting part. If you have honestly and prayerfully answered these questions and still believe you can move ahead, then do so, in full confidence that God is leading and He will open and close the doors (or change your desires) as He sees fit.

MEDITATE ON THESE PROMISES:

Psalm 32:8 "I will instruct you and teach you in the way which you should go; I will counsel you with My eye upon you."

Psalm 32:23-25 "The steps of a man are established by the LORD and He delights in his way . . . the LORD is the One who holds his hand."

Psalm 37:3-5 "Trust in the LORD and do good. Dwell in the land and cultivate faithfulness. Delight yourself in the LORD and He will give you the desires of your heart. Commit your way to the LORD. Trust also in Him, and He will do it."

Psalm 48:14 "For such is God, our God forever and ever: He will guide us until death."

Proverbs 3:5-6 "Trust in the LORD with all your heart, and do not lean on your own understanding. In all your ways acknowledge Him, and He will make your paths straight."

Proverbs 16:1-3, 9 "The plans of the heart belong to man, but the answer of the tongue is from the LORD. All the ways of a man are clean in his own sight, but the LORD weighs the motives. Commit your works to the LORD, and your plans will be established. . . .The mind of man plans his way, but the LORD directs his steps."

> "Dear God. Your will. Nothing more.
> Nothing less. Nothing else. Amen."
> (Bobby Richardson, former professional baseball player)

> The will of God will never take us
> where the grace of God will not follow.

© Dr. James M. Cecy, Fresno, CA.

APPENDIX FOURTEEN

DEVELOPING MY LIFE FOCUS

The following assignment should take quite some time and personal reflection to truly benefit. Write on a separate sheet, if necessary.

SOME FUNDAMENTAL QUESTIONS

Why do I exist?

- I exist "to glorify God and to enjoy Him forever." (Taken from the Westminster Shorter Catechism of 1647)

- I exist to fulfill "the purpose of God" in my generation.

Acts 13:36 "For David, after he had served the purpose of God in his own generation, fell asleep, and was laid among his fathers, and underwent decay. . ."

Why am I alive today? In what ways am I fulfilling/not fulfilling God's purposes? Am I fulfilled or just content?

Proverbs 13:12 "Hope deferred makes the heart sick, but desire fulfilled is a tree of life."

If life is like a book God is writing, what is He wanting me to do in this chapter? What do I expect the final chapters of my life to look like?

THE PROCESS OF CONVERGENCE

Convergence is that season of my life when my gifts, talents, experiences, dreams and opportunities begin to come together.

Proverbs 16:1-4 "The plans of the heart belong to man, but the answer of the tongue is from the LORD. All the ways of a man are clean in his own sight, but the LORD weighs the motives. Commit your works to the LORD, and your plans will be established. The LORD has made everything for its own purpose, even the wicked for the day of evil."

CONVERGENCE WORKSHEET

THE TIME-LINE OF GOD'S FAITHFULNESS IN MY LIFE

Philippians 1:6 "For I am confident of this very thing, that He who began a good work in you will perfect it until the day of Christ Jesus."

Mark down below or on a separate piece of paper a timeline beginning with the year of your birth. Using this timeline, chart out where, when and how you have most seen the Lord's power and guidance in your life. Be specific (with dates, events, etc.).

MY DESIRES AND DREAMS

Psalm 37:4 "Delight yourself in the LORD; and He will give you the desires of your heart."

Proverbs 20:5 "A plan in the heart of a man is like deep water, but a man of understanding draws it out."

What must I try to accomplish before I die?

MY IMPOSSIBLE DREAMS

Matthew 19:26 "With men this is impossible, but with God all things are possible."

Philippians 4:13 "I can do all things through Him who strengthens me."

What are those things I desire to do that seem impossible and are doomed to failure if God does not make it happen?

MY SPIRITUAL GIFTS

Ephesians 4:16 "...the whole body, being fitted and held together by that which every joint supplies, according to the proper working of each individual part, causes the growth of the body for the building up of itself in love."

1 Peter 4:10 "As each one has received a special gift, employ it in serving one another, as good stewards of the manifold grace of God." (cf. Romans 12, 1 Corinthians 12, etc.)

A Spiritual Gift Inventory is available in *"Men in Action: Equipping Men to Lead in the Home, the Church and the Community"* by James M. Cecy and Michael L. Wilhelm. Available at www.jaron.org.

My spiritual gifts:

MY TALENTS AND SKILLS   e.g. Paul, the tent-maker

Aside from my spiritual gifts, what talents has God given me and how can He use these to serve Him?

MY GENERAL EDUCATION

e.g. The testimony of Paul in Acts 22:3 "I am a Jew, born in Tarsus of Cilicia, but brought up in this city, <u>educated under Gamaliel</u>..."

My education and training:

How has my education and training equipped me to do what God is calling me to do? Be specific.

MY HOBBIES AND INTERESTS

My hobbies and interests:

How do I feel God can use these in serving Him? Be specific.

MY MINISTRY-RELATED EDUCATION

Acts 22:3 "I am a Jew, born in Tarsus of Cilicia, but brought up in this city, educated under Gamaliel, <u>strictly according to the law of our fathers, being zealous for God,</u> just as you all are today."

My Bible training, ministry training, etc.

MY MINISTRY EXPERIENCE

e.g. Paul's faith journey and testimony (Book of Acts, epistles, etc.)

List the ministry experiences God will use to equip me for the future:

MY VICTORIES

What are the areas in my life where I have seen God's power demonstrated? How have these impacted my life?

MY FAILURES

2 Corinthians 12:9 "And He has said to me, 'My grace is sufficient for you, for power is perfected in weakness.' Most gladly, therefore, I will rather boast about my weaknesses, that the power of Christ may dwell in me."

What are the areas in my life where I have seen God's power demonstrated in my weaknesses? How have these impacted my life?

Make a list of those things that will serve to remind me of God's grace and mercy, that if anything lasting is to be done, it is because of God and not me.

MY LIMITATIONS

Proverbs 16:25 "There is a way which seems right to a man, but its end is the way of death."

Proverbs 16:33 "The lot is cast into the lap, but its every decision is from the LORD."

Proverbs 19:21 "Many are the plans in a man's heart, but the counsel of the LORD, it will stand."

What might keep my dreams from happening? (e.g. physical, emotional, spiritual, financial, social, educational, etc.):

THE OPPORTUNITIES

Proverbs 16:9 "The mind of man plans his way, but the LORD directs his steps."

Colossians 4:5 "Conduct yourselves with wisdom toward outsiders, making the most of the opportunity."

Colossians 4:3 "...praying at the same time for us as well, that God may open up to us a door..."

List the opportunities available to me:

THOSE WITH WHOM I NEED TO CONSULT

Proverbs 15:22 "Without consultation, plans are frustrated, but with many counselors they succeed."

Proverbs 20:18 "Prepare plans by consultation. . ."

List those with whom I need to consult concerning these matters:

SPECIFIC OBJECTIVES

What am I going to do today?

What am I going to do this week?

What am I going to do this month?

What am I going to do this year?

Write a general summary of your life focus:

© Dr. James M. Cecy, Fresno, CA.

APPENDIX FIFTEEN

MY DAILY ACCOUNTABILITY WORKSHEET

When Daniel Webster was asked, "What is the greatest thought that can occupy a man's mind?" he answered, "Accountability to God." We also need to be accountable to each other: Proverbs 27:17 "Iron sharpens iron, so one man sharpens another." So we ask ourselves and each other these heart-felt questions:

1. Have I been faithful in the Word and prayer? Am I growing in my intimacy with God?

2. Have I been sensitive to the needs of my spouse? My family?

3. Have I been struggling with impure thoughts?

4. Have I been looking at questionable material (i.e. movies, TV, books, magazines, internet, social media, etc.) which would bring shame to the Lord?

5. Have I been alone with a man/woman in any kind of situation when my feelings became inappropriate or where others could have suspected something which would be suspicious?

6. Am I experiencing any physical problems? Eating right? Getting adequate rest and sufficient exercise?

7. Am I facing challenges in my ministry that are negatively affecting my physical, emotional or spiritual well-being?

8. Have I lied or compromised my answer to any of the above questions?

(A Personal Accountability Program with a number of accountability worksheets is available in *The Purity War: A Biblical Guide to Living in an Immoral World* by Dr. James M. Cecy. Available at www.jaron.org and www.puritywar.com.)

© Dr. James M. Cecy, Fresno, CA.

APPENDIX SIXTEEN

THE A.C.T.S. OF REPENTANCE

Many of us have mastered the art of cover up and denial. When our sin is discovered we resort to blaming, minimizing and rationalizing. The Bible is clear as to the steps to true repentance and restoration.

STEP #1 ADMITTING MY SIN
(Greek: *metanoeo* = bring it to the front of the mind)

2 Corinthians 7:9-10 "...you were made sorrowful to the point of repentance ("a change of mind," Greek: *metanoia*)..."

- **REFUSING TO HIDE MY SIN**

Genesis 3:10 "I was afraid . . . so I hid myself."

Job 31:33-34 "Have I covered my transgressions like Adam, by hiding my iniquity in my bosom, because I feared the great multitude, and contempt of families terrified me, and kept silent and did not go out of doors?"

Psalm 19:12 "Acquit me ("purge, clean out, make innocent," Hebrew: *naqah*) of hidden ("concealed," Hebrew: *cathar*) faults."

Psalm 139:23-24 "Search me, O God, and know my heart. Try me and know my anxious thoughts and see if there be any hurtful way in me, and lead me in the everlasting way."

- **STOPPING BLAMING OTHERS FOR MY SIN**

Genesis 3:12 "The woman whom You gave to be with me, she gave me from the tree, and I ate." (cf. James 1:14-16)

- **GRIEVING OVER MY SIN**

(cf. Ephesians 4:30; James 4:9; 2 Corinthians 12:21)

Psalm 32:1-2 "How blessed is he...in whose spirit there is no deceit."

Proverbs 28:13 "He who conceals his transgression will not prosper."

STEP #2 CONFESSING MY SIN
(Greek: *homologeo* = say the same words God would say about it)

Psalm 32:5 "I acknowledged my sin to You, and my iniquity I did not hide; I said, 'I will confess my transgressions to the LORD' and You forgave the guilt of my sin."

Psalm 38:18 "For I confess my iniquity; I am full of anxiety because of my sin."

1 John 1:9 "If we confess our sins, He is faithful and righteous to forgive us our sins and to cleanse us from all unrighteousness."

STEP #3 TURNING FROM MY SIN
(Greek: *epistrepho* = repent and return for filling)

Luke 22:31-32 "Simon, Simon, behold, Satan has demanded permission to sift you like wheat; but I have prayed for you, that your faith may not fail; and you, when once you have turned again (Greek: *epistrepho*), strengthen your brothers."
(cf. Psalm 139:23-24)

STEP #4 STRENGTHENING OTHER SINNERS
(Greek: *sterizo* = strengthen, minister to others)

Psalm 51:13 "Then I will teach transgressors Your ways, and sinners will be converted to You." (cf. Luke 22:31-34; Matthew 26:69-75; Romans 12:1)

The A.C.T.S. Process
- **Admit** it in my **Mind**
- **Confess** it with my **Mouth**
- **Turn** from it in my **Manner**
- **Strengthen** others as my **Ministry**

(Adapted from Chapter 41 of "The Purity War: A Biblical Guide to Living in an Immoral World." by Dr. James M. Cecy. Available at www.jaron.org or www.puritywar.org)

© Dr. James M. Cecy, Fresno, CA.

ABOUT THE AUTHOR

James Michael Cecy was born in Toronto, Canada in 1950, and moved to California when he was eleven years old. He entered the U.S. Navy in 1969 and served on the aircraft carrier, USS Kitty Hawk (CVA-63), during the Vietnam War. On November 17, 1971, the day he was released from active naval duty, God stirred his heart, and Jim trusted in Jesus Christ alone for his salvation. He quickly became an avid student of the Bible.

Jim was called to pastoral ministry in 1975, serving churches in California for over forty-seven years. He has served as the Senior Pastor-Teacher at Campus Bible Church of Fresno (formerly Campus Baptist Church) since 1995. He is known for his commitment to Scripture, his enthusiastic expositional teaching, and his passion to counsel and equip God's people locally and globally, especially as "a pastor to pastors."

Pastor Jim has a Bachelor of Arts degree in Speech-Communication from San Jose State University (1975). He earned his Master of Divinity degree in Bible Exposition from Talbot Theological Seminary (1978). In 1992, Jim received his Doctor of Ministry degree from Western Seminary (San Jose Campus) with an emphasis in pastoral counseling.

Dr. Cecy is the founder and president of JARON Ministries International, a training ministry that equips pastors, missionaries, chaplains, and Christian leaders around the world. It is based in Fresno, California. In addition to his domestic ministry in North America, Jim has traveled extensively in numerous countries. His training seminars have reached hundreds of thousands of people on five continents.

Jim has produced a variety of written, audio and video materials on a wide range of subjects, which are available in a number of languages through JARON Ministries International, Inc. (www.jaron.org) and his personal website (www.puritywar.com). His weekly expository sermons and messages are also available at www.campusbiblechurch.com.

Jim and his wife Karon were married in 1973. They raised three daughters and, since 1987, have cared for twenty-three foster-children. Two, even as adults, remain a part of the family. Jim and Karon are abundantly blessed with an increasing number of grandchildren.

ABOUT JARON MINISTRIES INTERNATIONAL

JARON stands for *Jesus' Ambassadors Reaching Out to Nations*. This ministry exists to:

> • build a team of Ambassadors of Jesus Christ (pastors, missionaries, chaplains and leaders) who will teach, disciple, and encourage disciples of Jesus Christ in the United States and abroad.

> • serve as a ministry of instruction and motivation to local churches and Christian organizations through pulpit supply, classroom instruction, conferences, seminars, retreats, short-term ministries, and special services.

> • produce and provide biblically sound and currently relevant written, audio and video training materials.

> • provide biblical, Christ-centered mentoring and counseling to those in need.

JARON is a registered non-profit organization (501c3) in the State of California. For further information about materials or seminars, please contact: JARON Ministries International, Inc., 4710 N. Maple Avenue, Fresno, CA. 93726 Ph: 559-227-7997 www.jaron.org

SCRIPTURE INDEX

OLD TESTAMENT

Genesis
1:18	34
25:8	15
35:29	15

Exodus
Chapter 4	74
17:7	97
32:29	38

Deuteronomy
5:24	71
10:12	52
16:17	88
26:17	88
26:18-19	88
29:29	109
30:15	18, 38

Joshua
1:8	112
24:15	18, 52, 102

Judges
Chapter 6	74

Ruth
4:14	85

1 Samuel
Chapter 1	124
12:23	121
14:38	73

2 Samuel
3:39	73

1 Kings
18:36	78

1 Chronicles
29:28	15

2 Chronicles
7:14	119
20:16-17	74

Nehemiah
1:6	77
1:11	38, 77

Job
8:9	17
14:1	17
14:5	17
14:16	63
17:11	59
27:8-10	117-118
31:33-34	147
35:12-13	119
42:17	15

Psalms
1:2-3	112
3:5-6	81
4:4	80
5:1-3	29, 42, 99-102
5:1-2	112
5:1	29, 30
5:2	30
5:3	30, 125
5:4-12	102
5:8	61

Psalms (continued)

10:1	120	57:8-9	27
17:3	69	59:16	27, 99
17:15	25	62:1	79
19:1-6	71, 109	62:5	80
19:7-11	39	66:18	118
19:7-14	39, 42, 109	73:28	28
		88:13	99, 100
		Chapter 90	16, 17
19:7-9	110	90:2	16
19:10	111, 112	90:4	16
19:11	112	90:10	16
19:12-13	112	90:12	16, 17, 43
19:12	147	90:14	16, 99
19:14	113	92:1-2	25, 32, 75, 80
22:1	120		
22:2	120	92:2	99
24:1	34	94:19	34, 36
30:5	73, 99	95:1-2	94
31:15	17	95:1	94
32:1-2	147	95:2	94
32:5	148	95:3	31, 95
32:8	65, 138	95:4-5	95
32:23-25	138	95:4	31, 95
33:11	63	95:5	95
35:10	44	95:6	96
37:3-5	138	95:7	61, 64, 96
37:4	140	95:8-11	97
37:23	60	95:13	21
37:23-24	66	96:2	56
39:4	17	96:4	21, 31
42:6	120	100:2	53
42:8	77	108:2	25
Chapter 46	100	109:7	118
46:1	28	113:3	32
46:10	35	118:1	97
47:1	94	118:24	27, 94
48:14	65, 138	Chapter 119	11
51:1-2	112	119:9-11	112
51:13	148	119:11	127
54:2	100	119:14	111
55:2	79	119:18	40
55:17	100	119:55	125

SCRIPTURE INDEX

Psalms (continued)
119:62	80, 125
119:72	111
119:103	111
119:127	111
119:147	25, 101
119:148	77
119:164	33, 42, 125
121:1-2	95
121:1-3	100
131:2	79
139:18	28
139:23-24	73-74, 113, 147, 148
141:1-9	82
141:2	78, 125
143:8	25, 99
145:2	31
145:18-19	118
150:6	44

Proverbs
3:5-6	138
3:5-7	60
3:24	81
11:14	137
13:12	139
15:8	118
15:22	137, 144
15:29	118
16:1-3	66, 138
16:1-4	140
16:3	6
16:4	57
16:9	60, 138, 143
16:25	64, 143
16:33	143
19:21	64, 143
19:23	81
20:5	140
20:18	144
27:1	60
27:9	137
27:14	26
27:17	145
28:9	118
28:13	147

Ecclesiastes
3:7	79, 82
4:11	12
11:10	17
12:10	13
12:11-14	143

Isaiah
1:10 ff	119
1:15-17	121
22:13	43
55:9	64
56:7	126

Jeremiah
Chapter 1	74
7:24	73
Chapter 29	117
29:11-14	126
29:11	100
33:3	126

Lamentations
Chapters 1-5	11
2:19	69
3:8-9	118
3:22-23	23, 102
3:40	69

Ezekiel
Chapter 34	122

Daniel
11:32	161

Jonah		**Malachi**	
Chapter 4	74	2:13 ff.	122
		2:14-15	137
Micah			
7:7	70		

NEW TESTAMENT

Matthew		**Luke**	
3:17	48	1:38	51
5:16	54	5:26	70
5:44-45	121	6:12	124
5:45	71	10:2	56
Chapter 6	118	11:1	117
6:5	119	11:9-10	124
6:7	124	12:19	43
6:9-13	115	17:3	106
6:9-10	115	18:1 ff.	126
6:10	115	18:1	124, 126
6:11	115	19:45-47	120
6:12	115, 123	22:31-32	148
6:13	115	22:31-34	148
6:24	137	22:45-46	125
6:33	137	22:46	26
6:34	19		
Chapter 7	117	**John**	
7:1	37, 108	1:5	47
19:26	140	1:12-13	45
21:12-17	120	10:4	136
21:22	124	10:10	45
24:44	137	13:14	107
26:69-75	148	13:34	37, 106
Chapter 28	74	14:7 ff.	120
28:19-20	56	14:13-14	101
		15:12-17	37
Mark			
1:35	25, 125	**Acts**	
3:31-35	136	13:36	43, 57, 86, 139
9:50	106		
11:24-25	125	17:11	13
11:25	123	22:3	141, 142
		26:16	51

SCRIPTURE INDEX

Romans
1:1	51
7:4	52
8:26-27	100
Chapter 12	141
12:1-2	137
12:1	148
12:9-10	37, 106
12:10	107
12:13	106, 107
12:16	105
12:18	36
12:19	46
13:1-7	137
13:8	122
14:9	106
14:13	37, 107
14:13-23	136
14:13	108
14:19	36
15:7	105
15:14	106
16:16	106

1 Corinthians
1:14-16	113
4:1	52
4:14	46
6:12-13	136
6:19-20	136
10:6-14	97
10:14	46
Chapter 12	141
12:25	107
15:58	46
16:20	106

2 Corinthians
5:17	45
5:20	54
7:1	46
7:9-10	147
12:9	142
12:21	147

Galatians
5:13	106
5:15	37, 107
5:18	71
5:19-21	137
5:22-23	137
5:26	37, 107
6:1	37, 105
6:2	105

Ephesians
1:3-14	128
2:8-9	55
2:19	54
4:16	141
4:26	123
4:26-27	36, 79, 108
4:30	73, 147
4:32	37, 105, 107, 123
5:1	46
5:15-17	135
5:16-18	135, 136
5:16	18
5:17	135, 136
5:18	71
5:21	105
5:22	137
6:1-3	137
6:19-20	52

Philippians
1:6	65, 140
2:3	37, 107
3:20-21	54
4:4-7	31, 137
4:6	123
4:13	140

Colossians	
1:7	46
1:9-14	128
3:1-5	45
3:5	46, 123
3:5-11	95
3:5-8	119
3:8-9	46
3:9	107
3:12	46
3:13	37, 105, 106
3:16	106
3:17	137
3:23	137
3:24	53
4:2	117, 123, 125
4:3	143
4:5	18, 83, 143

1 Thessalonians	
1:4	47
4:1	74
4:3-7	136
4:3	135
4:10	47
4:18	106
5:11	106
5:17	124
5:18	94, 135, 136

2 Thessalonians	
2:13	47

1 Timothy	
2:1	121
2:8	123
6:10-11	121

2 Timothy	
1:3	123
2:3-4	48-49
2:15	39, 113
3:16-17	110
3:16	12, 71, 137

Titus	
3:3	37, 107
3:5	55

Hebrews	
Chapter 3-4	97
3:13	83, 106
3:15	73
4:12	12, 111
4:13	112
4:16	29
10:22	29
10:24-25	71
10:24	106
10:25	106
12:1-2	117
13:8	7
13:15	94
13:17	137

James	
1:1	51
1:6	124
1:11	47
1:14-16	147
1:16	47
1:19-22	108
1:27	121
4:1-3	108
4:3	120
4:8	28
4:9	147
4:11	37, 107

SCRIPTURE INDEX

James (continued)		2 Peter	
4:13	60	1:1	51
4:14	17	3:9	136
5:4	121	3:14	47
5:9	108	3:17	47
5:16	37, 105, 106, 118, 120	**1 John**	
		1:9	148
5:17-18	124	2:15-17	136
		3:2	45
1 Peter		4:1	47
2:11	47, 54	4:11	47
2:13-15	135, 136, 137	5:14-15	101, 120
3:7	122	**3 John**	
3:17	135	1:5	47
4:8	37, 106	1:11	47
4:9	107		
4:10	106	**Jude**	
4:12	47	1:1	51
5:1 ff.	122	1:3	47
5:5	105	1:20	47
5:14	106		

Foreign Word Index

Greek

agapetos tou theou	*beloved of God*	*45*
epistrepho	*repent, return for filling*	*148*
extasis	*astonishment, amazement, ecstasy, wonder*	*70*
homologeo	*confess, say same words*	*148*
huperetes	*under-rower, servant*	*51*
metanoeo	*bring to front of mind*	*147*
metanoia	*change of mind*	*147*
ogkos (onkos)	*weight, hindrance, roadblock*	*117*
parodoxos	*remarkable, unexpected, incredible, wonderful*	*70*
phobos	*fear, awe, reverence, responding to power*	*70*
proskartereo	*strongly continue in*	*123*
sterizo	*strengthen, minister*	*148*

Hebrew

bachan	try, scrutinize, test like gold	72
cathar	hidden, concealed	147
dabak	cleave, cling, stick	52
damam	wait in silence, be still	80
gil	rejoice, shout for joy	27
hesed	lovingkindness, steadfastness	21
huwm	distracted, stirred	79
khadash	new, fresh	21
naqah	acquit, purge, clean, make innocent	147
'otseb	painful, sorrow-producing, idolatrous	73
ranan	sing aloud, creek	94
raphah	relaxing, sinking down, withdrawing	35
ruwd	restless, agitated	79
ruwah	split the ears with sound, shout	94
sabea'	full, abounding with satisfaction	15
samach	be glad, cheer	27
selah	pause, stop and ponder	82
temunah	form, attributes	25
yada	know intimately	35

Latin

carpe diem	seize the day	83
sola fide	faith alone	55
sola gratia	grace alone	55
sola scriptura	Scripture alone	55
soli deo gloria	glory to God alone	55
solus Christus	Christ alone	13, 55
tempus fugit	time flies	16
unum diem ad tempus	one day at a time	43, 66, 88

OTHER BOOKS BY DR. JIM CECY

• Anger the Worm in My Apple: Destroying the Rotten Fruit of Anger; Harvesting the Tasty Fruit of the Spirit (Also available in Czech and Polish).

• Mastering the Scriptures: A Self-Study Course in Effective Bible Study (Also available in Czech).

• Men in Action: Equipping Men to Lead in the Home, the Church and the Community (Co-authored by Michael L. Wilhelm).

• The Purity War: A Biblical Guide to Living in an Immoral World (Also available in Polish, Romanian, Czech, French, Bulgarian, Serbian, Ukrainian and Slovenian).

For information regarding these and other written, audio and video materials by Dr. Jim Cecy contact:

JARON Ministries International, Inc.

Jesus' Ambassadors Reaching Out to Nations

Equipping Leaders for Effective Service

4710 N. Maple Avenue, Fresno CA 93726
(559) 227-7997 www.jaron.org

". . . the people who know their God will display strength and take action." (Daniel 11:32)

www.ingramcontent.com/pod-product-compliance
Lightning Source LLC
LaVergne TN
LVHW051836080426
835512LV00018B/2907